The Politics of Multiracial Education

Routledge Education Books

Advisory editor: John Eggleston
Professor of Education
University of Keele

By the same author

Marxism and Education
Education, State and Crisis
Marxism, Structuralism, Education

The Politics of Multiracial Education

Madan Sarup

Routledge & Kegan Paul
London, Boston and Henley

First published in 1986
by Routledge & Kegan Paul plc

14 Leicester Square, London WC2H 7PH, England

9 Park Street, Boston, Mass. 02108, USA and

Broadway House, Newtown Road,
Henley-on-Thames, Oxon RG9 1EN, England

Set in 11 on 12pt Times
by Hope Services, Abingdon
and printed in Great Britain
by Billing and Sons Ltd
Worcester and London

Library of Congress Cataloging in Publication Data

Sarup, Madan.

The politics of multiracial education.
(Routledge education books)
Bibliography: p.
Includes index.

1. Minorities—Education—Great Britain.
2. Discrimination in education—Great Britain.
1. Title.   II. Series.
LC3736.G6S37   1986   371.97'00941   85-8297
ISBN 0-7102-0570-8

For my brothers and sisters

In memory of my mother and father

Contents

Acknowledgments

I work in the School of Education at Goldsmiths' College and help prepare students to become teachers. The department in which I work must have been one of the first in the country to have a compulsory course on multiracial education. After teaching on it for several years I decided to make the material used in my course into a short interdisciplinary textbook. As this is a general introduction to the subject, I discuss the work of many writers; their names are mentioned in the index and I am grateful to them. I would also like to thank the many people who have spent time with me, giving me emotional support and intellectual stimulus, whilst I have been writing this book. They include: Elsa Adamowicz, Peter Dunwoodie, Eileen Jebb, Barbara Klein, Heidi Mirza, Glynis Cousin, Bob Fine, Savitre Maharaj and Anne Kampendonk.

Introduction

Before you start reading this book I thought you might like to know a little about the author. I was born in India – in Simla. In the days of the Raj, when the weather became too hot in New Delhi, the British used to move to Simla every summer. It's a beautiful place – a small town on the side of a hill amongst the pine trees with panoramic views of the mountains, the Himalayas.

I don't remember my mother; she died when I was five. My father never remarried. I have been told that he was the first one in his village to pass what would now be called 'O' level English, and this enabled him to become a clerk in the civil service. He brought me to England when I was nine and when his leave was over he returned to India. I never saw him again. There are two stories about his death. Some say that, in the events of 1947, he was robbed and killed in his house. Others say that he was seen waiting at a railway station in the exodus and that he died of cholera.

And so I grew up in England, living in 'digs' from the age of fourteen. I remember my adolescence well. I can recall, for instance, the summer evening my girlfriend said to me that her parents had told her that she mustn't go out with me any more. I was puzzled and I asked her why that was. Her parents had said I was 'coloured'. Until that moment I had not been aware of the colour of my skin.

Since adolescence I have always thought of myself as an exile. It would be hard to explain why I have never felt at home in England – even after forty-four years. Perhaps this

1

book is an attempt to do that. I cannot call myself British. Well, why am I here, then? For most of my life I did not know. It is only in the last few years that the pieces have begun to fit together. The process began when I was studying Marxism and a friend suggested that I should read Lenin's little pamphlet on imperialism.

This helped me to understand why my mother died of ill health at the age of thirty-five; why my father died in the entirely avoidable partition of India; why he lived frugally so that I should have an 'education' in England. Sometimes I feel lonely; I have no real family life – my brothers and sisters are all in different countries, in France and Germany, Canada and the USA. I now know why millions of people became slaves, indentured labourers or exiles. I have begun to comprehend the forces that act on people to leave beautiful places like Simla in order to earn 'a living' in the advanced capitalist nation states of the West.

But now that I'm begining to understand, I don't cry any more.

During the last few years it has become clearer to me that capitalism is in the throes of an intense crisis that involves a far-reaching restructuring of capital and of capitalist social relations. There is a sustained attack on working-class living standards, on conditions of work, on the organizations of the working class, and on 'unproductive' state expenditure such as education.

In my book *Education, State and Crisis* I discussed some of the main manifestations of the crisis: the attack on progressive education, the increasing enforcement of discipline and, in response to youth unemployment, the emphasis on work-socialization. I contended that the current crisis involves an attempt to restructure social relations in fundamental ways, altering relationships between the public and the private, production and consumption, work and home, labour and leisure. There is an exacerbation of old divisions and opening of new ones between men and women, old and young, employed and unemployed, white and black.

Black and white . . . gradually I have realized that the Left in Britain does not seriously consider the problems, needs and aspirations of black people. And so I want to do something. Let me give some reasons for writing this book.

One: Britain is undergoing a political and economic crisis but it is also a crisis of the whole culture, of the society's sense of itself. The issue of race provides one of the most important ways of understanding how this society actually works and how it has arrived where it is. I believe that this understanding should be an essential component for all those interested in the social sciences.

Two: black people occupy a marginal role in education, employment and other spheres of social and economic life. This dismissal to the periphery is a generalized experience which constitutes a new and inferior form of citizenship, 'the new empire within Britain'. I wish to draw attention to this unjust situation.

Three: personal, institutional and state racism are major realities for black people in Britain. I use the term black to refer to all Afro-Caribbean and Asian oppressed people. The book shows how all these forms of racism are expressed in and through the educational system. It is my belief that all students and teachers should be fully aware of these issues. I hope to show that teachers *can* overcome the isolation and angry helplessness that many of them feel. I want to suggest ways in which they can challenge misconceptions and struggle more effectively for the creation of a multiracial society without exploitation.

Chapter 1

Multiracial education in the school

Introduction

Let us consider multiracial education from the point of view of teachers approaching it at the beginning of their careers. My first suggestion to teachers is that they should find out about the area around their school and do some careful, sensitive research into the background of their pupils. It is important to realize that black people do not form a homogeneous group. Among Afro-Caribbean and Asian peoples there are class, gender, age, religious and cultural differences. The 'research' should not be seen as an exercise in preparation of 'doing good'; teaching black kids is not some form of remedial therapy or social work.

My second suggestion is that teachers should find out if the school has a policy about race. Have guidelines been agreed upon by the staff? What is the school policy about racial abuse and harassment? What is one to do if one sees pupils writing racist graffiti, wearing fascist insignia, or distributing National Front leaflets? There are so many questions to consider that I shall divide what I have to say into sections that focus on pupils, teachers and the curriculum. These themes, briefly introduced here, are taken up and more fully discussed in later chapters.

The pupils

It seems to me that student teachers are too often inducted

into abstract principles and that it would be better if they gained an understanding through the study of specific cases. In this section I will try and deal with some problems about pupil behaviour that have been of concern to my students. My 'answers' to the questions that follow seem to me to be appropriate, but of course my responses cannot cover every instance. My 'answers' may be thought of as 'rules', but even when applying an apparently simple rule we have to make fresh decisions at each stage about what the rule 'really' means in the circumstances.

Should you treat black children the same as white children? Some people argue: if black children are different from white children (though not in any way deficient) then surely it follows that they should be treated differently from white pupils in school? Now, I believe that it is important for teachers to treat children *the same*. It is in the application of the principles of consistency and fairness that the problems arise. What does it mean to treat people 'the same'?

Too often inspectors, headteachers and others think of principles or rules unproblematically. People with a common-sensical or 'taken-for-granted' view don't realize that the application of rules is always problematic and is based on interpretation. We often use principles, or rules, in accordance with how we have defined the context; we often employ them 'retrospectively' to justify the decision already made. As Wittgenstein and others have pointed out, we use rules to retrieve sense in actions, we use rules in order to make sense of the world.[1]

In my view, to really treat black and white children 'the same', some form of extra attention should be given to black children. This is because black and white children are not in an equal relation in school. Compared with black children, white children have a hidden subsidy when they enter the classroom. This does *not* mean that black children are culturally deprived, or that they are deficient in some way. It is just that they have fewer opportunities to develop the specific skills and knowledges demanded by the school. Therefore, to help black children, there should be some 'positive discrimination' on their behalf, some affirmative action.

What should one do when black and white youngsters start

5

calling each other derogatory names? Yes, check it immediately. Stress what you think is right from the beginning. State your views, because sometimes pupils are 'testing' you. They want to know what you think and also what they should think. Many young children identify with their teachers and so what teachers think is important. It is to be hoped that a change in vocabulary may lead to a change in perception. At the same time explain to your pupils the ways in which language is racially biased. Consider the connotation of the word 'black' in common phrases such as these: Why are you giving me black looks? Are you in a black mood? Why have you got black thoughts? Am I on your black list?

'Think, too, about the ease with which the English language allows the terms of racial abuse to be coined: wog, frog, kraut, dago, spic, yid, coon, nigger, Argie. Can there be another language with so wide-ranging a vocabulary of racist denigration?'[2] It would be interesting to do an archaeological dig into white people's language, to find out how the meaning of words is overlaid by the effects of three hundred years of slavery, of imperialism and neo-colonialism. We must always be aware of the weight of history.

What should you do if your students tell racist jokes? Don't laugh; show your disapproval. Talk it through. For this to be done you need an understanding of the nature of jokes. Freud separated jokes into word play, puns, jests and innocent jokes on the one hand and tendentious jokes on the other.[3] The latter were usually of an obscene or hostile nature. He believed that innocent jokes, puns and jests derived their humour from an economy of expression. In tendentious jokes the lifting of repressed sexual and sadistic (aggressive-hostile) impulses provides the humour. It is because racist jokes (usually based on stereotypes) express aggressive-hostile feelings that they are hurtful; they belittle and degrade an oppressed minority.

Sometimes one does hear the argument that jokes about Asians or Afro-Caribbeans normalize the presence of blacks in British society, and that they demonstrate a certain degree of acceptance. But it is difficult to know how racist jokes can be funny unless you share the underlying assumptions.

What do you do if pupils see you as being trendy or

patronizing? And what if your colleagues label you as a troublemaker? Of course, if you are being radical there will be attempts to censor you, gag you, some people may even try to injure you. The only solution is the continuance of rational dialogue. As for the children you teach, they quickly come to know whether you care or not. If you care for people, you take an interest in them, you spend time with them. Children seem to know this. Sometimes what is important cannot be verbally expressed – it can only be shown.

What should you do when black kids try to exclude you? Some teachers feel threatened by the persistent use of a dialect they cannot understand, and their anxiety expresses itself in their attitudes and behaviour towards those pupils who use it. It is now generally acknowledged that the acquisition or retention of Creole in adolescence symbolizes the refusal to identify with white society. But why this refusal? It is felt that society, as at present constituted, *is not worth joining*. But, of course, it is not only black people that feel this. Dick Hebdige and others have pointed out that many working-class youth feel the same.[4] Punk, for example, originally expressed a distaste for an alienating consumer society.

But one *can* create an acceptable society in the classroom. This can be done by building up trust based on knowledge and understanding. After all, black people have been victimized for a long time and so they are mistrustful. Many of them have said to me that though white people often alter their vocabulary, their behaviour towards them remains the same. (Sometimes, contradictory messages are given at the same time, reminiscent of Bateson's 'double-bind'). In the short term one could say that teachers must be prepared to develop their cultural skills to interact competently with black pupils. And in the long run? Teachers, rather than concentrate all their energy on the containment of indiscipline, should attempt to change the system that causes it.

What should a teacher do if s/he is confronted with racism from students? Racism in the classroom must be confronted. By *racism* I mean the belief in, practice of, the domination of one social group identified as a 'race' over another social group identified as another 'race'. Racism

7

involves the belief that people can be grouped according to discrete races; the belief that some races are superior to others; and the belief that self-proclaimed superior races should control allegedly inferior ones. The teacher should demonstrate that these beliefs are false. It is a long, slow, and often very painful process, but many students will support the teacher if s/he carefully and patiently explains why some jokes, remarks, films, books and laws are racist and unacceptable.

If there is a racist attack in the school playground, would you bring the police into the school? I don't think I would. Young blacks are understandably sceptical of law and order because they experience racism and discrimination from the police. That a person is young, black and on the street appears to be sufficient cause for police action on many occasions.[5] In fact, wide-ranging and serious criticisms have been made against the police by the black community in recent years, but the British police have refused even to make racial discrimination an offence in their code of conduct, in spite of Lord Scarman's recommendations. The deteriorating relations between black youth and the police have undermined the official conception of the police as an impartial force administering the law on behalf of the whole community. It takes years to build up good relations within a school but they can sometimes be destroyed very quickly by calling in the police. Teachers should make clear to their students that racist attacks will not be tolerated. They must be dealt with immediately, otherwise more black children will lose trust in their schoolteachers.

The teachers

One of the reasons why many black students are rightly distrustful of white teachers is that they have been responsible for placing a disproportionate number of children of Afro-Caribbean origin in low streams, special schools, and now in 'disruptive units'. As Jones and Kimberley have pointed out; 'The widespread use of exclusion and suspension and disruptive units, which have recently been brought into play as methods of control, has by no means supplanted the subtler methods: "guided" option choice, long-term exclusion from lessons, teacher-condoned truancy, referral to educational psychologists and transference to special schools.'[6]

The school system itself is heavily implicated in fostering ways of thinking that make racism possible. The system encourages teachers to make assumptions that become self-fulfilling prophecies. In self-fulfilling prophecies something one expects to happen may occur only because it is expected to do so. In my view, most teachers see black children as a problem and have low academic expectations of them. It is not surprising that most of the educational research about black children shows low achievement and underperformance.[7]

It should be stressed, however, that such 'prophecies' are not inevitable. Some pupils can and do reject their teachers' judgments. Parents, schoolfriends and 'significant others' also influence the way pupils come to see themselves; their own experience of the wider society – through the mass media, for instance – may be of even greater importance. The findings of Michael Rutter's research are one such exception to the norm; he found that those black students that stayed on in sixth forms did very well. I think that this was probably because teachers defined these young people as keen and eager to learn, and the pupils' encouraging response in turn validated their teachers' attitudes.

In the past teachers have often ignored the powerful drive of the desire for recognition. They have also tended to take the curriculum for granted, not fully realizing how deeply it affects our view of other cultures.

The curriculum

People's views of the world arise partly out of childhood socialization, partly from the way in which the media portray other cultures and world events, and partly from the nature of the school curriculum.

Schools can covertly make racism seem reasonable through their teaching materials. The main problems are stereotyping, misinformation and ethnocentrism. We should therefore be aware of the way the curriculum is organized and the ways in which that organization leads us to think about knowledge and people. In most schools black culture and black history are ignored (if not denigrated) and I would argue that if you ignore the background, race and culture of children you are rejecting them and their identity.[8]

The racism in the school curriculum, like the racism in society, exists on two levels: the explicit and the implicit. School subjects are taught in an outdated and condescending manner; they often contain residues of imperialist ideology. Racist texts and images are overtly presented day after day – this is the 'explicit' level. The 'implicit' level is that of 'the hidden curriculum' which is based on assumptions and presuppositions that we are not aware of and which should be brought to light and questioned.

Let us take the teaching of geography as an example. Numerous important issues in this subject are left undiscussed.[9] Few textbooks consider questions such as, 'Why are poor countries poor?' In most texts the importance of other countries is seen only in terms of what 'they' produce for us. The effects of colonialism and the impact of imperialism on Third World economies are usually ignored. Teachers who are beginning to teach these topics face the following difficulty: on the one hand they want to bring to their pupils' attention the poverty and suffering of the Third World poor – the aspect that is highlighted by the media – and yet at the same time they want to emphasize the achievements of the countries of the Third World. The stress on deprivation can lead people to think of Asians and Africans as passive recipients rather than creative people who are being ruthlessly exploited. Images of Third World poverty and ethnocentric portrayal of 'developing countries' may affect both black self-image and white prejudice in this country.[10]

Structural racism

Through my work I meet many teachers and I have come to the conclusion that, if a multiracial society is to be constructed, then a change in their attitudes and *practices* is vital. Some teachers have no awareness of racism at all; there are others who are aware of racism but do not do anything active about racist practices in their schools. And then there are also those who know all about racism but whose efforts seem to be counter-productive. They are committed to helping black children and are really hard-working, but they fail to achieve very much because they see racism only as an individual, psychological problem.

It is difficult to blame these teachers because most discussions of multiracial education take place within a personality-orientated framework. Examples that come to mind are the Lawrence Stenhouse work where the emphasis is on individual feelings, or the work of Robert Jeffcoate on how respect for self and respect for others underpin a non-prejudiced society.[11] They mean well, but good intentions are not enough. In the chapters that follow I will demonstrate why this approach is inadequate.

I want to argue that racism must be tackled not only at the level of attitudes but also of actions, institutions and ideology. The individualistic psychological approach is attractive because it appears to be humanistic, concrete, direct and immediate, but in reality it deflects attention from the larger social system as a determinant of social inequality. If students are to become critically aware and autonomous they must know how they themselves and their schooling relate to society.

It is insufficiently understood that though racism can be the result of the conscious acts of individuals it can also be structural. I find it useful to distinguish three levels of racism: personal racism, institutional racism and state racism. Personal racism is that which exists on the level of prejudice in interpersonal relationships. Institutional racism can exist in the policies and practices of agencies and organizations. By state racism I mean racism that is built into the mechanisms, the policies of the state. Racism is built into the official policies (the successive immigration legislation) of the major political parties. Through state legislation racism has become respectable and permeates all aspects of social life at every level, in housing and social services, unemployment, police practices (the hunt for illegal immigrants, 'saturation policing') and schooling. Such racism, because it is legal, becomes accepted as 'normal'. The 'normal' becomes taken for granted. In the chapters that follow it will be argued that the fight against racism entails a

11

conscious effort to understand economic, political and ideological structures. Let us try and make the unseen visible.

Chapter 2

Racism and education

Introduction

It was suggested in chapter 1 that racism has been institutionalized in the education system and that it must be challenged. Multiracial education and multicultural education are *responses* to racism, but one problem is that these terms are often used interchangeably. What resonances does each term have?

A distinction has been made between denotation and connotation; denotation refers to the use of language to mean what it says; connotation is the use of language to mean something more than what is said.[1] The term 'multiracial' has quite a 'hard' connotation. 'Race' is controversial; it arouses anger, pride and guilt, and is often associated with conflict. You can adopt another culture but not another race. The term 'multicultural' has a 'softer' connotation; you have 'race riots' but not 'cultural riots'. Multicultural education is associated with the superstructural rather than the economic aspects of a way of life, with thought and consciousness, beliefs and customs – the curries people cook, the music they make, the dances they perform.

The term 'culture' is not a neutral one. On the one hand there is Matthew Arnold's definition of culture ('the best that has been thought and written') which refers to 'high' culture, usually the product of a society's literate and leisured elite. It therefore reflects their concerns and records their preoccupations. In this view the culture of the

13

oppressed, the culture of the working class, of women and of black people is usually regarded as inferior. But there is also the anthropological definition of culture which refers to ways of life which all groups have and which are of equal value. A curriculum statement which has 'culture' in this sense as its focus is a positive one.

It is not accidental that in most studies of culture economic position and social power are ignored. An emphasis on 'culture' tends to obscure certain issues such as the economic position of black people in relation to white, discrimination in employment and housing, differences in access to resources and in power to affect events. It is for this reason that I tend not to use the term multicultural and prefer to use the term multiracial education (MRE). In short, one of the reasons why there is no agreement over the use of these terms is because there is an ideological struggle over meaning. Different groups are contesting the definition of these terms.

From assimilation to cultural pluralism

The assimilationist model

Let us begin by approaching the topic historically to see how state institutions and agencies have imposed their views of multiracial education, and to see how the denotations and connotations of MRE have changed. Since the Second World War policies have stressed, in turn, assimilation, integration, and then cultural pluralism. Of course, in practice these policies often overlapped.

Ever since the 1950s teachers and administrators in Britain have tended to view black people as a problem. They were a problem because they were black; they were a problem because many of them could neither speak nor write English well enough to benefit from school education. Numerically, they allegedly posed an administrative problem for already overcrowded inner-city schools and a political problem which was expressed in terms of the fear that the whole character and ethos of the school would be radically altered.

14

From the early 1950s to 1965 multiracial education was largely based on an assimilationist model. There was a presupposition that immigrant groups were 'aliens' and that they posed a threat to the stability of schools and society. They should be absorbed into the indigenous homogeneous culture so that they could take an informed and equal part in the creation and maintenance of the 'host' society.

It was also presupposed that there existed a definable, shared value system into which all should be assimilated. One example of such thinking is 'the nation' as a unitary whole. There was also a belief in a stratified society in which pupils were placed hierarchically and ranked according to how well they had internalized traditional white, Anglo-Saxon, Protestant, middle-class values and norms.

In the assimilationist model and the policy that flowed from it it is taken for granted that black culture is inferior and that black values and beliefs are of secondary importance when considered against those held by white groups. And so it was assumed that the main educational problem of black people was their underachievement; the knowledge they brought to the school was inadequate. They therefore needed *compensation*. It was held that black parents inhibited the process of assimilation and that race problems would disappear with the death of the older generation. There was a belief that numbers were the problem and restriction the solution. The concentration of immigrants in certain areas was seen as a threat which could interfere with the educational progress of white pupils.

During this period, the mid-1960s, testing was taken to 'prove' the educational inferiority of the black child. Blame was placed on family instability and the cultural level of the home. Attention was focused on language. A black child speaking a language from a black country was seen as backward, not as actually or potentially bilingual. Assimilationist policy, it seems, has to deny the existence of a viable culture in those to be assimilated.

For the policy makers, then, immigrants posed an alien threat to the British way of life. And so it was insisted that black children be taught English as quickly as possible, and they were 'bussed' to outlying schools to avoid undue concentration in any particular school. It was believed that assimilation could be achieved through the controlled dispersal of black pupils. But, as Chris Mullard has pointed out, to assimilate, for whites, means to stay the same; to assimilate, for blacks, is to discard their identity and all that culturally defines their existence.[2]

The integrationist model

With the failure of the assimilationist policy there was a change; from 1965 to the early 1970s multiracial education was based on an integrationist model. Compared with the model out of which it evolved, the integrationist model is less crude. Integration was defined as 'not the flattening process of assimilation but an equal opportunity accompanied by cultural diversity in an atmosphere of mutual tolerance'.[3]

During these years concern was expressed about the large number of Afro-Caribbean children in educationally sub-normal schools; dispersal policies were officially abandoned, and there was the beginning of 'Black Studies'. This type of education was based on the view that black children had low self-concepts. It was claimed that there was a relationship between their low self-concept and low achievement, and so an attempt was made in some schools to try and change their self-concept through the introduction of Black Studies in the curriculum.

To put it bluntly, 'social pathology' was the justification for compensatory programmes. This view assumed that black pupils in British schools were 'problems': that they suffered from culture shock, negative self-images and identity crises, and that their language structures were inadequate and inhibited learning. Blame was thus placed on the students, but educational theorists went further – they traced the cause of these problems to the black families. This racist 'common sense' justified educational practices which were remedial, compensatory or coercive.

It is probable that the narrow emphasis on Black Studies, for example the playing of steel bands, merely solidified racial stereotypes ('We all know they are good at music, but . . .'). Black Studies was a subject for black youth – it didn't have any status. Black Studies were certainly not allowed to affect the academic, high-status subjects in the curriculum which most schools foster and legitimate. This sort of MRE has quite rightly been vigorously attacked by many black educationalists. We will be looking at an influential critique of Black Studies by Maureen Stone in chapter 4.

Another approach was provided by those curriculum developers who emphasized the discussion of social issues with the teacher as the neutral chairperson. I am thinking particularly of the work associated with Lawrence Stenhouse.[4] There was an attempt to overcome stereotypes through the discussion of topics such as prejudice and discrimination. Pupils expressed their feelings whilst the neutral teacher listened but did not participate. The assumption underlying this approach was that if only people *talked* ignorance would be dispelled and harmonious relationships would develop. But does this sort of 'liberal' discussion, without any intervention by the teacher, lead to a change of attitude or does it just harden prejudices?

Under the liberal gloss the integrationist policy differs little from the assimilationist's belief in a politically and culturally homogeneous society. Within this model cultural diversity is tolerable so long as it neither impedes progress to 'integration' nor explicitly challenges the cultural assumptions of Anglocentric white society.

Cultural pluralism

In contrast to the assimilationists' view of our society as being politically and culturally homogeneous, the advocates of cultural pluralism maintain that our society consists of different groups, which are culturally distinctive and separate under the political authority of a neutral state.[5] If the integrationist model is in fact a more sophisticated and liberal variant of the assimilationist model, then the cultural pluralist model is in effect a more refined version of both.

'Cultural pluralism' is a term that has become overworked and empty. The main thing wrong with this model is its assumption that all groups within the plural society possess roughly equal amounts of power. It is taken for granted that all groups are able equally to assert pressure on the state and negotiate with its agencies for the maintenance of cultural equilibrium.

But blacks do not possess anything like the same amounts of power as the dominant whites. It is clear that black groups in a white society could not develop their cultural traditions without the unconditional approval and encouragement of white society as a whole and of white power groups in particular.

The sociology of 'race relations'

Having described three models of multiracial education, I will argue that the policies that flowed from them were heavily influenced by the growth and popularization of a sociology of 'race relations' and a psychological approach to multiracial education. I will now critically examine these 'discourses' which are shaping a racist public policy, and will argue that multiracial education in the hands of political conservatives has become a form of co-option and control.

As the views of the sociologists of 'race relations' have shaped public policy at every level from government offices to school staff-rooms, it is important that we examine their assumptions. What is their view of black people and what type of account do they give?

It is usually assumed by such writers that Afro-Caribbean cultures are 'weak'. They often refer to 'culture stripping' or 'cultural castration' which African slaves supposedly underwent during slavery. And so it is said that the slaves lost their languages, religions and family kinship systems, being left with no alternative but to learn their masters' language and to ape their values and institutions. Writers like Stanley Elkins, for example, have argued that because the master was the only 'significant other' in the slaves' world and because there were only a limited number of roles available to them, the slaves became physically and psychically dependent upon their master.[6] They came to identify their interests with those of their master.

This type of account neglects the activities of the slaves themselves, their cultural institutions which provided a source of alternative values and practices. There is now ample evidence that the view of Afro-Caribbeans as totally 'acculturated' is a false one. The slaves did retain elements of their African heritage (this can be seen in aspects of their languages, religions and music), and these formed the basis of the re-creation of their culture. Moreover, where the slaves adopted elements of European cultures, they did so on their own terms. In contrast to the dominant view of the docile slave I want to stress the fact that black people actively participated in the creation of Caribbean cultures.

The second assumption in many studies is that the black family is pathological. The fiction we are told is that there was a destruction of family life among slaves; and that the family is an unstable institution because of the proliferation of common-law unions and high rates of illegitimacy. The lack of social control in the West Indian family is said to lie in the fragmentation of family structure in slavery. 'Race relations' sociologists tend to stress the 'identity crisis' of Afro-Caribbean youth and, more recently, intergenerational conflict within black families.

The family is important not only because it is here that culture is reproduced, but also because it is the principal site where black people are recognized as having a degree of autonomy. Now, it should be remembered that there is no 'natural' form of household organization; the 'family', as we know it, is a specific form of the European bourgeoisies. There is no doubt that sex/gender systems are different in Afro-Caribbean societies, but this does not mean that they are pathological or inherently inferior as we are told by the sociologists of 'race relations'. In fact, during slavery family life was highly valued; it offered black people companionship and hope for the future. The family is particularly important for black people at the present time because it is the principal site where they have a degree of autonomy.

Furthermore, sociologists of 'race relations' tend to emphasize the differences between the cultures of ethnic minorities and the 'majority society' and to assume that these differences interfere with effective communication. The emphasis on differences prepares the way for blaming blacks themselves for the discrimination they suffer; it is their *difference* that generates 'natural' hostility, their cultures that create the many possibilities for misunderstand-

19

ing. As the sociologists focus on mutual misunderstandings, questions of power are never explored.

Moreover, there is a failure to comment upon the impact of Western imperialism. The poverty of the 'Third World' countries is seen as the result of their 'backward' and 'rigid' social and cultural institutions. In this way two core images of black people are sedimented into working common sense: they are either 'children needing protection' or 'brutal savages'. The oppositions superior/inferior, responsible/ irresponsible, mother/children, civilization/barbarism provide a reserve of images that racists can use. It is important to challenge these stereotypes, but it should be remembered that racism is not limited to a struggle over forms of representation. A struggle over images can easily disguise the social relations of domination and subordination in which it is situated and which it reproduces.

In short, the sociology of 'race relations' focuses on culture and ethnicity and carefully avoids any discussion of politics and economics. The research of these sociologists is based on social-democratic, pluralist assumptions in which the state is considered to be neutral and the capitalist system is taken for granted.

I have argued so far that the theories and policies of multiracial education have been largely determined by the racist assumptions and 'findings' of the sociology of 'race relations'. Now, all theories have unexamined assumptions or presuppositions, but what is important here is that there is a close relationship between the sociology of 'race relations' and *policy making*. Wherever policies are being formulated to deal with black people the influence of the 'race relations' sociologists can be discerned. As Errol Lawrence has written, 'In a situation where state racism has intensified, it is disingenuous for policy-orientated researchers to expect that their racist and patriarchal conceptualizations of black people will not be of interest to the state institutions which oppress black people.'[7]

The psychological approach

The usual story we are told is that Afro-Caribbean children

'fail' at school because of their 'weak' culture, their pathological black family backgrounds, 'identity crises' and negative 'self-image'. You will have noticed that these explanations are psychological. I will now make some criticisms of the psychological approach which has dominated multiracial education and argue that it serves an ideological function: it serves to deflect attention from the racist structures and practices of the British state.

As an example of this approach I will examine *The School in the Multicultural Society,* a collection of readings prepared for an Open University course. I am disturbed by the views of many so-called educational experts who continually stress the inadequacy of the black child:

> A white middle-class child for example, with confidence in his cultural inheritance, will clearly not have the same sorts of needs as a black working-class child with unsure or ambiguous feelings about his identity and ancestry.[8]

One of the authors, Alan James, writes;

> The hope is that ethnic-minority children, if they acquire a more positive evaluation of those factors (skin colour, home life, communal history and traditions) which give them their own identity, will have higher aspirations for themselves.[9]

James is here repeating the myth that black children do not have a positive evaluation of themselves and that this affects their identity and their aspirations. One of the reasons that some black people do not have high aspirations is not that they are not capable of realizing them but because they reject many of the expectations and values of white society. I believe that black people have a more positive evaluation of themselves than the author realizes. Blacks do not have ambiguous feelings about their identity. They know exactly who they are. I will justify these assertions in the chapters that follow.

There are many other examples in the book of the tendency to 'blame the victim':

After all, in school the language, clothes (e.g. turban), dietary customs and beliefs they [the parents] have given him are ignored if not regarded (e.g. Jewish holidays) as a nuisance! No wonder many Muslim or Sikh teenagers experience severe crises of identity.[10]

I agree with the author that schools often disregard the beliefs and customs of their pupils, but what I object to is the notion that black people have an inadequate sense of self. This view, that black people suffer from negative self-image, poor self-concept and an insecure sense of identity, became the 'common sense' of the late 1960s.

The 'liberal' attitudes of this period can be seen in an essay, written in 1971, on social studies in a multiracial society:

The usual teaching methods encourage the view (often shared by West Indian pupils) that Africans were indeed lucky to be rescued from savagery! One of the problems faced by black youngsters is that their formal education here and in the West Indies and America has done nothing so far to challenge this view, and is one cause of the phenomenon of self-hate. The reaction away from this has produced a growing demand for so-called Black Studies, a demand which urgently needs to be met. Reviewing the materials available, one finds the best is very much orientated towards the British view, and this is not good enough. At best, they might engender pity for the slave, who is seen through the eyes of the nineteenth-century liberal reformers. Our problem was to get beyond pity, to respect for the person.[11]

I will not comment on the reference to the 'self-hate' of black people, but the recommendation that the solution is respect for the person should be noted because this implies that the problem is a *moral* one. MRE is also defined as being about morality by Robert Jeffcoate, one of the co-editors of the book. In the first essay he makes a distinction between 'instructional' and 'expressive' objectives. Broadly speaking, this distinction corresponds to the distinction between cognitive and affective domains. What astonishes me is how this distinction is then used to define MRE. Jeffcoate writes; 'Multiracial education is primarily affective, about attitudes and dispositions.'[12]

In such definitions of MRE there is concern for the evolution of a just multiracial society, but the motor of change is always the individual rather than the collective, the psychological rather than the social. According to this view the aim of MRE, the affective objective, is respect for self and respect for others.[13] I believe that the problem is neither a psychological nor a moral one. The stress on these discourses has an ideological function. It follows that if there is a psychological problem the remedy is individual therapy and that, if the problem is a moral one, well, we can all resolve to be 'kinder' to our fellow human beings – tomorrow. Psychological and moral discourses are thus used to displace economic and political explanations – they distract attention from the exploitation and oppression of black people.

Schools and society

A characteristic shared by many of the writers in *The School in the Multicultural Society* is the assumption that the school is an independent, autonomous institution. This can be seen most clearly in the essay by Robert Jeffcoate, who writes;

A school's selection of objectives in multiracial education will be significantly affected by two factors which are themselves interrelated – its value system or educational philosophy and its definition and analysis of the situation (problems, needs and so on) which it finds itself confronted with. The simple relationship between a school's stated objectives and its overall educational philosophy has long been recognized.[14]

Now, I would argue that a school is *not* able to select objectives as if it was independent of other institutions and processes that determine the educational system. At times Jeffcoate seems to realize this and he concedes; 'The school, after all, is not a valuefree institution; nor could it hope to be, no matter how open its relationship with the surrounding community.'[15]

Note that outside the school there is a 'community' – a word which has connotations of a unified, harmonious group. The idea that the school may be surrounded by fragmented groups, races and classes that are in conflict with one another is not considered. Schools, in my view, are interrelated with other institutions in complex, uneven and contradictory ways. What is missing in this sort of 'social democratic' perspective is any notion of the school as an ideological state apparatus.[16] It takes the independence of the school for granted and does not question its ideological character. In the thinking of these theorists the determinations of the school by capital and state have no place.

The aim of social-democratic educators is to foster an approach which stresses the absence of prejudice, the ability to suspend judgment, to argue rationally and to change one's mind in response to evidence or argument. This approach often propagates some abstract notion of 'rationality' or of 'objective scientific understanding', but it does not realize that so-called scientific understanding is itself political.

It is typical of such writers that they make an appeal to 'democracy'. Alan James's essay concludes;

> Such an education can only be provided in a context where children are encouraged to articulate their own ideas, to question . . . and, as they grow, to take an increasing part in the practice of democracy – in debate and negotiation, and the election of representatives within school, and in informed and critical use of sources of information and opinion and society – the press, television, newspapers, libraries . . . democratic education and education for democracy are inseparable, and must stand at the core of the curriculum for life in a multicultural society.[17]

This description of democracy, in terms of debate and negotiation, the election of representatives, refers to a bourgeois conception of democracy: parliamentarianism. James makes no reference to the relationship between political democracy and the state, or the relationship of the state to capital. Nor does he mention the fact that traditional notions of British tolerance and fair play have broken down and 'democratic' institutions have failed to protect black people. I would argue that the 'informed and critical' use of sources of information is not enough – in a socialist democracy it is the *control* of the press, television, newspapers, of all the means of production, that is important.

The role of social policy

It will have been noticed that there are remarkable similarities between the sociologists of 'race relations' and the psychologists of multiracial education; there is a fundamental agreement between their ideas and those of official agencies. The reformism of these social democrats leads them to formulate and support government social policy.

Social policy in Britain is largely based on the premise that Afro-Caribbeans suffer from weak family units and that young people are alienated from British society, in part, by the failure of the family unit to provide support. The implication is normally that there are strong generational differences, perhaps exacerbated by the differing expectations and reference groups adopted by migrants and their offspring. If the cause of a problem is understood as psychological and/or 'cultural' and if it is thought to require welfare intervention, then the culture is seen as flawed. In this way social policy has confirmed marginality, or possibly even magnified it.

The same general process can be found in the growing concern for the 'special needs' of black children. There has been readiness to respond with alacrity to the proposition that Afro-Caribbean children have 'special needs'.

The policies of government agencies seem to be based on the supposition that the real problems immigrant minorities face are cultural differences, newness and unfamiliarity. Government agencies have a consensus that the major problem is not that of discrimination but that of 'disadvantage', giving rise to 'special needs'. Discrimination is an act perpetrated on a victim; 'disadvantage' is a malady caused by a difference from, a non-acceptance of, 'British' culture.

To sum up: the idea that blacks have a negative self-image is an ideological mechanism to control them. In the process of ideological dissemination some people came to believe such assertions. I have argued that racism has been approached by many 'experts' as if it was a matter of attitudes, opinions, beliefs and prejudices. These immediate surface-manifestations are usually considered in a psychological perspective that is assumed to be neutral and scientific. Attitudes and beliefs of individuals are seen as something to do with differential perceptions of other people, as emanations of good and bad *feelings*. From this position it is easy to interweave another thread into the ideological warp: the notion that racism is a problem of morality and that its solution is respect for the person.

MRE, like the education system itself, is a site of political and ideological struggle. In MRE there are many who want to incorporate black people into a society that is fundamentally unchanged. I have called this view 'social democratic'. Social democratic experts often propagate the view that school is an independent, autonomous institution that can challenge the racism of the surrounding 'community' by instilling into pupils a respect for persons, and bourgeois 'democracy'.

But it should be remembered that even with a multicultural curriculum the problem of racism will not disappear from schools because the sources of racism are not only the teachers, the curriculum, or the educational system. The fundamental reasons for the disabilities of black people are the racist attitudes and practices in the larger society itself. Racism is inherent in all institutions of the state.

Chapter 3

Children and racial attitudes

Introduction

In the last chapter I suggested that multiracial education is dominated by a social psychological perspective which focuses upon individuals and their subjectivities. David Milner's work is an example of this type. His book *Children and Race* (1973) focussed on the development of racial attitudes in young children. The author remarked that the book enjoyed an undeserved celebrity because it was the only contribution of the kind but 'it has needed revision for some time'. And so there is a new book, *Children and Race: Ten Years On*.[1] After giving a brief exposition of this book I will make some comments as it is an influential and *representative* example of social psychological thought in multiracial education. It will be argued that one of the features of this discourse is reformism, a political position which amounts to changing one small thing – so that everything can remain the same.

Socialization

For social psychologists like Milner the socialization process is the most important 'determinant' of prejudice. In the course of socialization society teaches us not only ways of doing things but also ways of seeing – that is, its values. At

27

first, it is the parents that define the child's world; they explain that world and define its limits.

Socialization occurs through several overlapping processes: direct tuition of explicit attitudes, indirect tuition and role learning. Besides individual or personality determinants there are also cultural influences on children's attitudes. It is suggested that we should look closely at reading material where the symbolic black/white, bad/good theme occurs. Milner says that in language, literature and art white is conventionally used to depict all things good and pure and blackness to denote badness and evil, but he offers no critical analysis of these forms. He merely quotes from books written by Hugh Lofting (Dr Dolittle), Enid Blyton (Noddy) and W.E. Johns (Biggles) and states that they contain an unmistakable message: black people feel shame about their blackness and desire to be white. It is ironic that Milner's own research replicates this view.

Milner did some research into children's racial attitudes and identity using doll and picture tests. In previous research,

> the dolls have been simple peg-like figures, or at the other extreme, the over-glamorized, commercially produced toys which have been equally unrealistic. In this study the basic figures used were realistically proportioned scale models, with skin colour, eye colour, hair colour and type, and facial features appropriate to each of the groups they represented. The children were required to choose between an English doll and a West Indian or Asian doll in response to questions put by the interviewer. . . .[2]

> In response to the standard identification question, 'Which of these two dolls looks most like you?', 48 per cent of the West Indian and 24 per cent of the Asians maintained that the white figure looked more like them. When asked, 'If you could be one of these dolls, which one would you rather be?', 82 per cent of the West Indians and 65 per cent of the Asians indicated the white doll rather than their own group figure. In addition, 35 per cent and 20 per cent respectively misidentified one or more family members when asked, 'Which one of these two dolls looks most like your mother/brother/sister?'[3]

Most of the empirical research discussed in the book is based on the view that black people introject white attitudes which hold them to be inferior.[4] The argument, in other words, is that black people are constantly receiving an unpleasant image of themselves from the behaviour of whites. This view is widely held. It is often said in the sociology of education for instance that it is because of their negative self-concept and poor self-esteem that black children in British schools come to see themselves as failures and are non-achievers. And so, for Milner, misidentification in the doll tests is an index of a basic ambivalence on the part of black children concerning their identity. To support his case he utilizes quotations from black 'authorities' who suggest, for example, that 'Negroes have come to believe in their own inferiority'.[5] To put it in another way: black people are ashamed of their own colour because white society has forced them to accept its own appraisal of them.

According to this ethnocentric psychology there is a choice of evils: in each direction there lies anxiety and lowered self-esteem. By identifying with whites the blacks are insecure, they are vulnerable in the sense that they develop acute anxiety and mental illness; by identifying with blacks they incorporate with their own self-image disparaging elements which damage self-esteem and may lead to emotional disturbance. I do not understand why Milner devotes such a lot of space in his new book to these early accounts of 'the psychological predicament of black people'.[6]

Maureen Stone, whose work will be discussed in the next chapter, has made a valuable critique of the doll studies. She suggests that if one thinks of how black dolls are depicted in children's literature and television it is not surprising that children should respond to black dolls in the way Milner reports. Moreover, it is usually a *white* researcher that asks black children which dolls they prefer. Stone asks:

> Can choice of dolls really indicate race preference in a child? Do children regard dolls in the same way as they regard people? Is it a realistic and valid inference to make that choice of doll indicates how children feel about themselves and their race? Or is it a function of fashion,

of the market place and what is being offered generally to children in their everyday lives?[7]

I agree with Stone that school achievement is basically related not to self-concept but social class. Ultimately, it is power, not self-concept, that counts.

The thesis that black people introject white attitudes which hold them to be inferior is, of course, too sweeping, it lacks specificity. I believe that *some* black people introject *some* white attitudes and that in certain situations the pressure of the dominant values can be very strong. One of the reasons why I object to the introjection theory put forward by social psychologists like Milner is that it is one-sided; he does not fully understand the *dialectical* nature of all human relationships.[8]

Black consciousness, black power

Milner repeats many tired old clichés drawn from an era which predates the growth of black consciousness. Realizing that the stereotypical views of conventional psychology are now being challenged, he plaintively asks; 'Who would have predicted that black people would *choose* to identify with their African roots? Who would have agreed that black is beautiful thirty years ago?'[9] Yes, the emergence of African states, the growth of the Black Power movement and liberation struggles throughout the world have reminded black people of their hidden history, their rich cultural heritage, and have aroused a fierce racial pride.

Milner believes that his first study revealed a degree of white-orientation in black British children on a par with the earlier era of American findings. Within five years a further study showed a substantial decline in 'misidentification'. By the end of the 1970s the phenomenon had almost disappeared. A researcher like Milner is now in a difficult theoretical position. Either he has to admit that his early work on black identity was wrong, or he has to say that because of changes in black consciousness his work is now of no relevance.

He argues that the early studies of black children's identity were valid though they exaggerated the amount of psychological damage black children suffered because of the prevailing 'pathological' view of 'black psychology'.[10] This admission is only made in one sentence in a book which gives a lot of space to the pathological view of black people. I would argue that it is precisely because of the dominance of this 'deficiency' model that the work is pernicious. Ten years have passed and Milner still believes in 'inferiorization'. It is obvious that he has not been to any political meetings in Bradford or Brixton lately. He wants to have it both ways: to recognize a dynamic model of change and yet, at the same time, assert the importance of his own empirical research.

In the first doll studies the vast majority of black children said they would rather be the white figure. This may have been simply a recognition that to be white in this society is to be valued and privileged. Milner concedes that black children are now quite clear about their racial identity and view it positively. I believe that they always have been — the black child is surrounded by black parents, teachers and others who evaluate him/her as highly as white parents evaluate their children. Moreover, blacks do not merely internalize guilt or blame, they understand the political and economic situation and they know the cause of their subordination.

Some criticisms

I want to argue that Milner's lack of understanding arises out of the nature of his discourse and his politics. His political stance is cautious and ambivalent: 'This is not the place for an all-embracing discussion of the aims of education,' he writes, 'the issue of how far education is, or should be, an agent of social change and a vehicle for achieving social equality, is one which has taxed educational theorists and policy makers for many years. . . .'[11] A chapter on race and the black child concludes with a revealing quotation: 'It is in this crevice between the heightened sense of personal worth and the sharpened perception of relative status that the seeds of inter-group hostility will germinate.'[12] The concepts used here are significant: the emphasis is on status rather than class and there is 'inter-group' hostility rather than class struggle. It is my contention that Milner's discourse is based on an ethnocentric social psychology, a Weberian bourgeois sociology and reformist politics.

This is exemplified in the policies that he thinks should be applied in schools. Milner suggests that we need to educate white children against prejudice and at the same time foster a positive sense of radical and cultural identity among black children. As racism is a problem that whites have, anti-racist teaching is vital, but the second proposal shows that he still does not understand that black children have a sense of racial and cultural identity. I repeat: black people know exactly who they are – their problems are not to do with self-image and identity but with exploitation and oppression.

Since the 1920s, social psychology has been concerned with attitudes, with the emphasis on the innate character and abilities of people rather than social and historical factors. Milner is aware of the limitations of the research into attitudes and prejudice; generally, rather poor correlations have been found between people's measured attitudes and observed behaviour. He knows that prejudices and stereotypes have expedited the oppression of groups through history but the book gives the impression that prejudices are inherent, ahistorical and universal.

There is, then, a confusing ambivalence in Milner's work. On the one hand he realizes the dangers in the psychologists' concern with 'prejudice' so that it is sometimes seen as a psychological phenomenon with a life of its own; something that people 'are' or 'are not', an affliction of their personality. He rightly points out that

> the explanation of prejudice in terms of individual motivations and conflicts . . . carries with it dangerous implications for social action against racism. If we conveniently locate prejudice in the 'disturbed' personalities of individuals, we may mistakenly believe that the resolution of their personal problems solves the issue.[13]

On the other hand, he wishes to 'ground the account on a more thorough foundation of social psychology than before'.[14] But if racial prejudice is usually, and on the whole, the individual manifestation of political and economic forces (as he says it is) then, surely, the most valuable approach would be to study those forces which are the *causes* of racism? Why does he persist in using a starting point that is so obviously inadequate? Why are racial attitudes not presented in any historical, educational, or political context? (He does not provide a history of multiracial policy and practice in Britain till the final chapter.) Milner's book shows that, though a decade has passed, the author's views, despite his protestations in the introduction, have not really changed very much at all. The book also serves to remind us that there have been very few concrete advances in multiracial education over the last ten years. For example, the Rampton Committee could not identify a single teacher training institution which had succeeded in providing a satisfactory grounding in multicultural education for all students. In my view most teachers, if they are not overtly racist, see themselves as being non-racist. In spite of the growing literature on the subject many of them have low expectations of black pupils and still use derogatory and limiting stereotypes. Not only does there exist a big gap between the awareness of race issues and any widespread commitment to action in this country, but it seems to be getting wider.[15]

Though Milner's book contains a lot of empirical case studies it provides no theoretical understanding that would be of value to those committed to anti-racist teaching today. With his psychological approach Milner can say nothing about how multiracial education is being used as a state strategy to defuse and recuperate black resistance in schools and society. He wants to do good but he is completely unaware of the bitter conflict between those who want to use multiracial education to preserve the status quo and those who see it as one of the means of bringing about a better society.

Chapter 4

The education of the black child

Introduction

In the last chapter I said that dominated cultures are usually defined as inadequate, deficient or flawed. This legitimates intervention – a social or educational policy then operates to confirm marginality or possibly even to magnify it. A well-known example of this ideological process is the (still) fashionable argument that the educational failure of working-class and black children is due to poor self-concept and that, if this is treated, they will achieve more at school. I agree entirely with Maureen Stone's view that it is a false and dangerous argument based on incomplete and unsound assumptions and biased reasearch findings. In this chapter I will present her thesis and then make some criticisms of her work.[1]

Black self-concept and multiracial education

The idea that self-concept is to blame for black or working-class underachievement is based essentially on theories which regard black and working-class culture as deficient and which assume the internalization of the negative views by these groups themselves. Theories which explain the black child's low achievement as being due to poor self-image, family background and other social-psychological factors put the schools under increasing pressure to respond

34

to these needs by developing pseudo-therapeutic programmes. It is said that black children would achieve better in schools if their self-concepts could be 'improved' or 'enhanced'.[2] This argument was influenced by three tendencies in education: a humanistic psychology based on the work of Kelly, Maslow and Rogers; a philosophy of education which stressed individual development and growth; and pheno-menological sociology with its stress on individual meaning and subjective experience as a means of defining reality. Many teachers in urban schools are using teaching methods based on these theories. Schooling has now become a form of therapy with teachers acting as counsellors and social workers.

However, the introduction of 'Black Studies' and teaching methods based on developing relationships with children may actually increase educational inequality through their emphasis on mental health goals (increased self-esteem) at the expense of academic achievement.

Stone examines the research on black self-concept and self-esteem which has been undertaken in Britain since the 1970s and finds it inconclusive and contradictory. In her view there is no basis in fact for the belief that black children have poor self-esteem and negative self-concept. The 'therapeutic' approach looks potentially rewarding but it may not be an advance at all, because it mainly serves to obscure the real issues, which are of power, class and racial oppression. There is now a vast body of evidence showing that working-class and black families have much less access to power, to resources of every kind, than middle-class children. By ignoring the social structure and its reflection in the school system, these theories are potentially very damaging to the education of the working-class and black child. The emphasis on 'self-concept' has thus become a way of evading the real and uncomfortable issue of class and privilege in our society.

Whilst social scientists have been busy proving that black people have negative self-images based on white stereotypes, blacks have been living in accordance with *their own* 'world-view'. This point has been expressed, amongst others, by black intellectuals as Négritude, by radical activists as Black Power, and by poor and dispossessed Jamaicans as the Rastafarian faith.[3] The psychological theories ignore the fact that people derive the means to sustain a sense of self from many sources and do not only rely on negative and hostile views as their source of information about self. Black people do not simply introject the negative views of the black society; through political, social, literary and musical styles people create alternative sources of selfhood.

One solution offered to the problem of black under-achievement is multiracial education. Stone asserts that there is an unexamined assumption that MRE is 'a good thing', not dissimilar to the assumptions about progressive education in the early 1970s. She suggests that the aims of multiracial education are tied in with the cultural deprivation theory which aims to compensate working-class children for being culturally deprived (of middle-class culture) and black children for not being white. It takes schools and teachers away from their central concern which is basically teaching or instructing children in the knowledge and skills essential to life in this society.

The question arises whether MRE represents anything more than a misguided liberal strategy to compensate black children for not being white. Stone believes that the materials published under the MRE label are often so patronizing and ethnocentric that it probably has the effect of encouraging the very attitudes it seeks to change. The school system has never reflected the culture of the majority of children in this country who are working-class. Why then this concern to reflect the culture of small sections of that class – West Indian and other minority group children?

Supplementary schools

What cannot be overstressed is that there is real bitterness in the West Indian community (which Stone concentrates on) at the way the school system is seen as treating black children. There are large numbers of black children in schools for the educationally subnormal and there is an overwhelming concentration of blacks in the remedial and lower streams of comprehensive schools.[4] While many schools try to compensate children by offering 'Black

Studies' and steel bands, black parents and community groups have started organizing Saturday schools to supplement the second-rate education which the school system offers their children. The development of Saturday schools mirrors in many respects the socialist Sunday school movement of the late nineteenth century, which offered to working-class children the means to foster a self-image based, not on therapy or charity, but on hard work, disciplined study and the will to succeed.

It is well known that in British schools Afro-Caribbean pupils are seen as boisterous, hyperactive children who present teachers with problems of classroom discipline. But the teachers in Saturday schools told Maureen Stone that they had no problems with discipline. Their overriding concern was not with 'relationships' but with teaching the children basic skills. The children came because they wanted to learn; they knew what was expected of them and they got on with it.

In the state system West Indian children continue to underachieve (for whatever reason), lagging behind white working-class British children in tests of attainment in school subjects, but Stone's research shows that community-based supplementary school projects have in them children who exhibit more positive attitudes to school, less negative attitudes to teachers, and higher aspirations than children in a comparison group.

The main point of Stone's book is that teachers who emphasize self-concept, self-esteem and enjoyment do so at the expense of more concrete objectives. The central recommendation of her study, therefore, is for the use of more formal methods of teaching West Indian children. Schools should be places for acquiring skills and knowledge.

Gramsci's name is briefly mentioned at the conclusion of the book where she states that he was against the reflexive self-indulgence of highly individualistic, romantic liberals. He argued against a child-centred view of education because he knew that such emphasis would result in an almost totally ignorant and illiterate working class.[5] Gramsci knew that for the working class to succeed they had to produce intellectuals capable of mastering an elite culture and turning it to their own use.

Comments on Stone's argument

It is important to make some criticisms of Stone's thesis because, though her book focuses on the education of the West Indian child, she contends that the argument can be extended to the whole of working-class education.

Her book is deservedly influential because of its trenchant criticisms of MRE. She suggests

> that MRE is conceptually unsound, that its theoretical and practical implications have not been worked out and that it represents a developing feature of urban education aimed at 'watering down' and 'cooling out' black city children while at the same time creating for teachers, both radical and liberal, the illusion that they are doing something special for a particularly disadvantaged group.[6]

Now, of course, MRE may well be all those things – at the moment. She is quite right to say that it is patronizing and ethnocentric; in the hands of some teachers it often is. But I think that Stone is one-sided, she does not have a conception of MRE as a terrain of struggle between contending forces where some groups are trying to contain a potentially progressive movement within a reformist framework, whilst other groups are struggling to make it politically radical.

The present characterization of MRE is 'steel bands and Black Studies'. Stone, however, wants to emphasize the acquisition of 'basic educational skills' through formal methods. But she treats this unproblematically. Freire has shown that in the teaching of skills (like reading), form and content are related and cannot be separated.[7] We know Stone favours 'formal methods' but she never states what 'knowledge' is; nor does she disclose what her epistemology (theory of knowledge) is. Is the curriculum, for example, a structure of socially prescribed knowledge, external to the knower, there to be mastered? Or is it something to do with learners making sense of their life-world?

There are other 'silences' in Stone's book; she says nothing about state racism, or what schools should be doing about racism, the school curriculum, the alienation of pupils and the attitudes of teachers. Whilst I agree with Stone's argument that teachers should not be further encouraged into teaching methods based on romantic ideas of 'self-realization' and 'self-fulfilment' to the detriment of their pupils' interests, I don't think that this should necessarily mean a stress on formal methods. I believe that teaching should not be polarized into the 'child-centred' and 'formal' approaches. Such dichotomies usually lead to simplistic debates. I believe that we should develop a concept and a practice of a type of teaching that overcomes the limitations of both 'child-centred' and 'formal' approaches so that a dialectical unity is possible between the subject of knowledge (the learner) and the object of knowledge (the curriculum). This is the moment when it is possible for the learner to integrate apparent contradictions and to transform them into a unity which provides a new and deeper understanding of the world.

Let us now turn to the question: what does Stone see as the educational aim for black children? She writes;

> Within contemporary urban British society the West Indian community is faced with a school system which traditionally has offered a second- or third-rate service to working-class people and traditionally English working-class people have accepted that service; at best making the most of it to get out and move up, at worst simply accepting and suffering what was offered.[8]

In short, Stone sees education as a useful instrument for blacks to 'get out and move up'. Nowhere in the book is there a reference to challenging the system, or trying to change the basis of society in a socialist direction. This is one of the reasons why I regard Stone's politics as reformist.

Stone makes reference not only to *social* mobility but to *international* mobility. She believes that West Indians are not trapped in the way that the English working class is trapped and that a bright West Indian child who worked hard could succeed and get to be internationally mobile:

> I have constantly 'drawn on my knowledge' of West Indian life to understand certain processes – for example mobility – in terms of West Indian working-class life.

'Mobility' here means not simply moving up on the social ladder but moving on (to another country if need be) in order to move up the social scale.[9]

She says that one of the reasons why there is no West Indian middle class to speak of in this country is the fact that successful people and their children simply move on 'back home', or to North America, and increasingly parts of Africa.[10]

I think that this part of Stone's argument is false; because of the changes in production, namely the use of electronics and computers, *less* labour power is now required. Moreover, because of the worldwide crisis of capitalism there is an increase in unemployment and a general tightening-up of immigration laws. 'Third World' countries have limited financial resources with which to buy 'skilled labour' from elsewhere. Black labour is trapped here – there is nowhere for it to go. Most young blacks in Britain have no knowledge of their so-called 'country of origin'. Rejecting the 'social mobility' option, they are either refusing to do 'shit work' and contracting out, or they are gradually becoming politically radicalized. As I have suggested, Stone is a reformist and so it is not surprising that the theme of political mobilization is absent from her work.

Stone makes the (somewhat odd and ambiguous) assertion that her own position 'is somewhere in between the structural-functional and phenomenological extremes'.[11] She mentions the word 'class' occasionally, but she does not use a marxist mode of analysis. In my view economic arguments are central to the discussion of educational issues. The lack of a marxist analysis means, amongst other things, that she is unable to discuss capital (and its relationship with the state) and how it exploits the social divisions of race, class and gender for its own advantage.[12]

In the controversy between Gramsci and Gentile (the fascist minister of education who tried to push Italian education in a 'child-centred' direction) Gramsci argued on behalf of instruction – but it should be observed that this was fifty years ago in the context of Italian fascism. When Stone refers to Gramsci she makes a selective and pragmatic use of his ideas, referring only to his educational views and not to his political theory. Gramsci's views on education were related to the task of creating organic intellectuals, who would serve the revolutionary working class.[13] In his view there is a dialectical unity between education and politics; in Stone's book, however, there is a separation between them – there is a focus on education but the politics disappear. This 'split' between education and politics is a pervasive feature of liberal democratic thought.

To recapitulate, in the above section I have made the following criticisms of Maureen Stone's argument: firstly, her critique of MRE lacks an understanding of class struggle; secondly, the emphasis on the teaching of skills by formal methods ignores the dialectical relation between the human subject and the object of knowledge; thirdly, the stress on social mobility leads to political reformism; fourthly, the notion that skilled black people are internationally mobile is false; fifthly, the absence of economic categories leads to limitations in her analysis; and, sixthly, her use of Gramsci shows a misunderstanding of his work.

In spite of these inadequacies Stone's work does have merit and has helped me in several ways. It raises for me the crucial question: how do we create a socialist transformation of education? Stone writes that the development of supplementary schools mirrors some of the socialist educational movements in the nineteenth century. These schools represent, for her, the only real example of working-class community involvement in education at the present time. But in my opinion her stress on the teaching of basic skills and knowledge by the use of formal methods (which is exactly what the Right is demanding) in no way challenges the status quo. There is no reference in her work to struggles over the *forms* of education or the *hierarchies* that exist within the system. It is time that questions concerning the development of socialist alternatives in education were put on the agenda.

Chapter 5

Knowledge, the curriculum and racism

Introduction

In the last chapter I stated that though Stone's central concern is that black people should have knowledge essential to life in this society she does not see the importance of epistemology. Of course, this does not mean that she does not have a theory of knowledge. It is quite clear from her book that she has a view but it is implicit. She sees the curriculum as a structure of socially prescribed knowledge external to the knower, there to be mastered – a view rather like that of the 'liberal' philosophers of education, Richard Peters and Paul Hirst. Stone argues that only by mastering the traditional curriculum will more West Indian children have that basis of choice which many middle-class people take for granted. As her work lacks any consideration of epistemology I will begin by briefly outlining three ways of looking at knowledge: the view of the 'liberal' philosophers of education, that of the radical sociologists of education, and a marxist view. I will then focus on institutionalized racism in the curriculum by examining one school subject. (I will look at geography but I could have selected any school subject.) Finally, it will be argued that socialist teachers must construct a new kind of curriculum.

The view of the 'liberal' philosophers of education

What should be taught in schools is a matter of great

42

controversy. This is partly because our notion of the curriculum is often based upon our view of the nature and purpose of knowledge in our lives. The dominant view of knowledge amongst British philosophers of education is associated with academics such as Richard Peters and Paul Hirst.[1] They believe that human beings have slowly differentiated out various types of knowledge: there are forms of knowledge, fields of knowledge and practical theories. *The forms of knowledge* refer to seven kinds of conceptual structure: mathematics, the natural sciences, the human sciences, moral knowledge, religious knowledge, philosophical knowledge and aesthetics. Three points should be noted. Firstly, each form of knowledge has its own distinctive concepts. Secondly, the concepts within a form of knowledge are logically related to each other. Thirdly, each form of knowledge has its appropriate evidence, its own test of validity.

Peters and Hirst argue that everything we know is within these domains; there is no knowledge outside them. These domains are autonomous; sometimes, of course, one domain uses the concepts of other domains. For example, scientists use mathematical concepts but scientific truth is different from mathematical truth. The use of concepts from one form of knowledge by another shows the interrelationship of knowledge. Though there are interlocking relationships between the forms of knowledge, nevertheless they are logically different and distinct.

The *fields of knowledge* refer to domains where several forms of knowledge constitute a subject, for example, geography. The *practical theories* include law, medicine, engineering and teaching.

Learning, it is said, is like making a jigsaw puzzle; concepts are learnt by relating them to other concepts. And, of course, people can do the puzzle in different ways. Hirst writes that the 'liberal' philosophers' approach is about content, not about method, which means that child-centred education could be included in this model. In his lectures, however, he appears to be highly critical of progressive methods that are used in child-centred education.

In short, the 'liberal' view of education insists that all children be introduced to the forms of knowledge. Under-

43

standing depends on grasping these differentiations. The young must be *initiated* into the forms of knowledge. To be educated means to have mastered one or two of them. The forms of knowledge are ways of understanding and embody the ideals of 'rational argument'. In other words, the study of the forms of knowledge is initiation into rationality. This disciplined understanding leads to the development of the person.

What criticisms can be made of this way of looking at knowledge? The 'liberal' philosophers' view of education neglects the personal experience of the pupil and the role of interpretation in everyday life. I would argue that if knowledge is imparted as if it was something external to the knower it becomes alienating for many pupils. Moreover, the philosophers assume that knowledge, like their own philosophizing, is neutral and that education is also. They stress that education involves changes in *mind*, but neglect (the need for) changes in society.[2] In my view their support for the status quo is as much a political act as opposing it. The philosophers neglect problems of power and do not ask: why is some knowledge preferred rather than another? How is it selected, by whom and for what purpose? These are the questions that were asked by their leading antagonists, the 'new' sociologists of education.

The view of the 'new' sociologists of education

The powerful and pervasive view of the philosophers of education was challenged by a group of radical sociologists, Michael F.D. Young, Geoff Esland, Nell Keddie and others.[3] Their work, a reaction against the positivism of the social sciences and the elitism of a rigid society, was based on the principles of social phenomenology. Whilst the philosophers' 'model' tends to stress teacher-directed learning, the dominant norms and values, the phenomenological mode emphasizes the actors' rationality, the validity of pupils' experience and their view of the world.[4] This model of teaching and learning is much more 'symmetrical' than the first one.

The sociologists underlined the point that knowledge is

socially constructed and that the characteristics and status of different school subjects could be changed. It was hoped that by a change of consciousness of schoolteachers education could be altered, that schools would shift their focus from the written to the oral, from the theoretical to the practical, and the individualistic to the collective. To demonstrate these possibilities the sociologists used many anthropological studies which raised questions about the validity of our categories, our views of what is rational/irrational, intellectual/ emotional, religious/scientific.

In this view of knowledge the problem of imposition was avoided only to be replaced by another problem: relativism. If every culture is as good as any other, why choose one rather than another? Michael Young and his associates believed that education was political, but as their views were based on Schutz rather than Marx they etherialized the concept of power. The sociologists neglected the role of the dominant class, of capital and the state.

A marxist view of knowledge

A marxist view of knowledge holds that there is a material world which exists independently of our consciousness, and which can be known by consciousness. (Consciousness, however, cannot exist independently of matter.) In this view, which is called dialectical materialism, there is a unity of thought and matter, but this is not a unity or identity which excludes all difference and contradiction. Appearance and reality, thought and matter, the subjective and the objective are both opposed (different) and also united (identical). They are opposites which exist in unity.

The opposition, the distinction of thought and reality, is to be seen in the fact that they do not always and necessarily coincide. Our ideas about reality can be mistaken and false. It is held that opposites interpenetrate and pass into each other. Matter is transformed into thought and thought into matter. There is constant transformation from one to the other. In the processes of perception and knowledge we appropriate the objective world and transform it into consciousness and thought. In practical activity we translate our subjective purposes and intentions into reality, we realize them and embody them in things. The interpenetration of thought and reality is a familiar and everyday phenomenon: in eating and drinking, for example, we appropriate and incorporate the material world and thus sustain our conscious and subjective being.

Marxists reject the empiricist view that experience can be a source of knowledge. They believe that there is much in human knowledge that is not given directly in the outward and immediate appearance of things. Experience tells us only of particulars, and no matter how extensive it is, it can never inform us of what is universally or necessarily the case. Thought is the means by which we can penetrate beyond immediate appearances and the given data of the senses, and grasp the deeper levels of reality: the underlying structures.

Sometimes appearance conceals reality but it should also be acknowledged that reality is revealed to us in and through appearances. Consider the example of dreams. In the past it was sometimes thought that dreams were merely false and illusory visions but Freud showed that they could be interpreted. The dream is the distorted reflection of aspects of the dreamer's reality, and the very distortions reveal facts about the unconscious wishes and desires of the dreamer.

Initially we may take the immediate appearances that things present for reality. But, gradually, through the process of knowledge we come to distinguish appearances from reality. When we have done this we come to understand appearances as appearances which reveal the reality which underlies them and which is manifest in them.

A marxist view of schooling

Most marxists would argue that knowledge is related, in some way, with economic and political power. They are interested in the relationship between knowledge and ideology. How is it, for example, that some categories rather than others become dominant or come to be defined as 'rational' or 'acceptable'? A marxist view (to put it very simply at this stage) suggests that schools, on the whole, transmit knowledge, or withhold it, in the interest of the dominant class. It could be said that the school system establishes certain thought habits in a generation. These tend to become accepted as absolute by those acquiring the culture.

There is a growing body of opinion which sees the educational system not as a means by which social inequality may be overcome, but as a means by which it is perpetuated. Many marxists support the contention that the school is an ideological state apparatus concerned with 'social reproduction', with reproducing society as it is, with its hierarchy of knowledge, of power, and its graded labour force.

One such view is expressed in Samuel Bowles and Herbert Gintis's book *Schooling in Capitalist America*.[5] What I find valuable in their work is that they redirect attention from the alleged failings of the individual (in terms of IQ, ability, motivation, low self-concept, etc.) to the failings of the educational system in capitalist society. Their theory of social reproduction is concerned with the political economy of schooling, and is often referred to as 'the correspondence theory' of schooling because it asserts that the educational system prepares students to be future workers on the various levels of the hierarchy through a *correspondence* between the social relations of the school and the social relations of capitalist production. The authors stress the creation of specific personality dispositions and argue that the content of school knowledge is of little importance – what is really significant is *the hidden curriculum* This refers to the transmission of implicit norms, values and beliefs through the underlying structure of the curriculum and, more particularly, the social relations of the classroom and the school.

The correspondence theory of schooling ('the school is functional for capitalism') has been severely criticized because of its reductionism. It cannot account for the variety of responses of teachers and pupils to the structures of the school. It says nothing about how the dominant ideology is often rejected, resisted or redefined by teachers and students. The theory does not illuminate how ideological hegemony is mediated both within and between schools and other institutions. In other words, the correspondence theory does not do justice to the struggles and contradictions that exist in the schools and in society.[6] Bowles and Gintis have a monolithic view of the school as a conservative force, a view reminiscent of the functionalist tradition which they sought to challenge, which means that they have an unduly passive view of human beings.

Many writers have drawn attention to the fact that schools cannot be seen unproblematically, as Bowles and Gintis tend to do, as sites of social reproduction. Paul Willis, for example, has written about 'the lads' – the youngsters who most need personal development but actively reject education.[7] According to Willis, their responses are not ignorant but are realistic bets about their chances in class society and how best to approach a future impoverished in manual work. In his study 'the lads' are sceptical of qualifications because they know no amount of certification amongst the working class will produce more jobs or more mobility – it just produces social legitimation for those who seem to have succeeded.

'The lads' resist anything to do with mental work. This acts as a kind of inoculation against mental competencies and aspirations required for 'cissy' middle-class jobs. The vibrancy of the counter-school culture manages to associate academic 'underachievement' with worldly precocity. Masculinity is very important in that it helps to discredit mental life and, by being given some displaced meaning and dignity, leads to an acceptance of heavy work. Willis makes the point that individual working-class kids may succeed in education – never the whole class.[8]

The younger generation of American educationalists like Michael Apple, Jean Anyon, Henry Giroux and others are sympathetic to Willis's approach which could be called 'contested reproduction'.[9] They argue that contradictions exist in society and express themselves in different types of schools. Jean Anyon, for example, has written about how the lack of successful ideological incorporation of working-class pupils is a possible source of disruption in the reproduction cycle.[10] In the middle-class school the emphasis on individual success is likely to be contradicted by the realities of a rapidly contracting job market. An emphasis on creativity and meaning in the affluent professional school may come into potential conflict with demands increasingly being made on the newer professional classes by the bureaucratic rationality of the corporate state.

In the above section I have drawn attention to three limitations in Bowles and Gintis's work: their disregard of the overt *curriculum*, their underestimation of *resistance*, and their lack of understanding of the nature of *contradictions*. The point that needs to be stressed is that contradictions do not just 'explode' but they have to be seized by committed people. This is what is already beginning to happen. Black communities and groups have begun to struggle to redefine what constitutes education. The school curriculum, one of the means by which racism is perpetuated, is being increasingly questioned. It is to a discussion of the curriculum, the contradiction between educational and race relations policy, and the resistance of blacks to these policies that I now turn.

Racism in the curriculum: a case study

Racism, according to a well-known definition, is

> a set of attitudes and behaviour towards people of another race which is based on the belief that races are distinct and can be graded as 'superior' or 'inferior'. A racist is therefore someone who believes that people of a particular colour or national origin are inherently inferior, so that their identity, culture, self-esteem, views and feelings are of less value than his or her own and can be disregarded or treated as less important.[11]

In the current (cultural pluralist) approach in schools it is assumed that racism is merely a matter of individual ignorance, and that racial prejudice and racial discrimination will come to an end through an education in cultural diversity. There is an emphasis on the removal of racial stereotypes from school textbooks, but some unconscious racism always seems to slip through. Here is an example from a textbook designed for use in teacher training:

> In the Caribbean people live together in crowded kin-group communities, and they share one another's hopes,

49

fears, joys, sorrows, troubles and all family occasions. When they come here they find a climate which is cold, wet and highly unpredictable; they have to live most of their lives indoors, and there is no common 'yard' where all the street can congregate and engage in idle chatter. They begin to experience a pace of life which is greatly removed from the *dolce far niente* of the tropical Caribbean; its speed and unchanging incessant routine are at first strange, and to some quite terrifying. If we suffer from 'colour shock', they suffer from climate and culture shock.[12]

Blacks 'naturally' crowd together, their language is 'chatter' and because it is 'idle' it explains why they are technologically and culturally backward. This is the sort of stereotypical thinking that is still common in schools today in spite of the efforts of many progressive teachers. There have been a few improvements but on the whole the school curriculum, based as it is on white cultural values, is something black youth cannot identify with. I will demonstrate this by looking at a representative example of institutionalized racism: the teaching of geography and its treatment of the 'Third World'.

In a review of recent geography-teaching material Dawn Gill found that the content is still strongly influenced by what could be called a colonialist perspective: the importance of other countries and peoples is seen primarily in terms of what 'they' provide for 'us'.[13] Examining textbooks she discovered that many of them present Europeans as people who have organizational ability and are scientific and efficient business people who build roads and railways. Non-Europeans are presented as dependent peoples who have houses and roads built for them and are given jobs which enable them to survive; they are without talent or skills and are the passive recipients of aid.

Of the twenty syllabuses studied, Gill found fourteen that presented the developing world exclusively in terms of problems. Typically, the problems faced by the 'Third World' are presented as internal to those countries. There is no suggestion that solutions may be political or influenced by global economic systems. Moreover, most of the syllabus writers took a Western model of development for granted. To 'develop' seems to mean 'to become more like Britain and the USA'. It was found that most of the books lack any kind of explanatory structure which would enable pupils to make sense of the world as it is and to understand how it got that way.

In this context it is important for teachers to show that 'Third World' countries may have options between different kinds and models of development, and that the debate about these options is fundamentally a debate about politics and ideology. To sum up the link between geography teaching and MRE: in most textbooks the explanatory framework within which problems are analysed is usually one which fosters the view that individuals are responsible for creating the poverty in which they live. I believe that this framework should be replaced. The poverty in most of the countries of the 'south' should be seen within the context of global politics and of capitalism as a world economic system.[14] Such a perspective would help undermine the negative attitudes towards Third World peoples that are so pervasive at present.

It is important that pupils realize that the disparities in wealth and development are not 'natural' but are 'social', that they are *created*. In order to understand the world it is necessary for young people to comprehend the *processes* by which inequality came into being and by which it is perpetuated.

Changing the curriculum

What can teachers do about the institutionalized racism in the curriculum, the syllabus and the textbook? I would maintain that when a curriculum is being constructed the perceived reality of children should be taken into account. We must listen to what pupils are saying. Some white children may be asserting that 'the Paki's are taking over the shops, our houses, our jobs'; 'the blacks are a drain on the social services, they sponge off the welfare state'; 'blacks commit more crime than white people'. If these views are part of the perceived reality of the pupils, then the content of the curriculum must include information on such issues.

The Rampton Report states that teachers should examine critically the textbooks and teaching materials they use and take into account their appropriateness in today's multi-cultural society. Usually teachers interpret such a statement to mean that they should censor biased material. I want to suggest that to do this may be less useful than to give children the concepts and skills which would enable them to recognize *the underlying assumptions in a text.*

In the past the analysis of school textbooks was largely descriptive; sociologists set out to explore why educational texts took the form they did and why some messages were transmitted rather than others. It was found that many social science textbooks expressed a static view of society; they used a functionalist perspective and stressed social harmony and stability and negated the value of conflict. Through their tacit assumptions most of the textbooks legitimated the existing social order.[15]

In the last few years, however, there has been a great increase in the approaches and techniques available; our understanding of textual messages has been aided by the insights of post-Saussurean theory, semiology and structuralist theories developed within marxist criticism, and I believe that some of these approaches should be taught to young people.[16] They should be given the opportunity to develop the desire and the capacity to control the apparatus of meaning-production, of which school knowledge is one aspect.[17]

We need to explore which aspects of school knowledge are reproductive in their effects and which are potentially transformative. Perhaps, as an example of the former, we should question the use of packaged curricula. There may be a relationship between the tendency towards the increasing use of commercially manufactured curricula in schools and the changing modes of control within capitalist societies. Michael Apple has suggested that the form which these teaching materials take contributes to the formation of the type of 'possessive individual' appropriate to the current stage of the development of capitalism.[18] It is for this reason that I believe that teachers should be encouraged to make teaching materials for their own purposes rather than use packs of commodified knowledge produced by experts in international marketing.[19]

I believe that we should try and construct a curriculum that reflects the reality that in Britain there are many racial and cultural groups. I feel that all boys and girls should have some teaching of a multiracial character even if they live in areas where there are few immigrants. Additionally, this teaching should not be contained within specific 'courses' but the whole curriculum should be permeated with MRE. It is often said that teachers should promote 'tolerance' towards different cultures in Britain but this is not enough. There is a need for positive anti-racist teaching if a multiracial society is to be created in this country.

It would be better if we spent less time thinking about the 'underachievement' of blacks and more time thinking about how the education system is failing them. Instead of compensating the pupils let us try and change the schools. One way in which we can do this is by working collectively with colleagues to change the content of the overt curriculum, and by teaching our students techniques by which they can analyse the implicit assumptions and the social relationships underlying the hidden curriculum. The present educational system is not immutable, neither are the social relationships embodied within it.

Curriculum, contradiction and resistance

Let me now try to pull together some of the threads of the argument. When I described the move from assimilation through integration to the currently fashionable concept of 'cultural pluralism', you may have felt that this seemed a liberal, humanitarian advance. But I would argue that there is a contradiction between what appears to be happening in curriculum policy and what is happening in terms of the state and its race relations policy. The contradiction is this: at the same time as an apparently liberal advance in schools there has been a change in the balance of state response from a liberal humanism to increasing repression. Since the end of the 1960s there has been a shift to more direct, overt and authoritarian forms of social control in race relations. This can be seen in successive pieces of immigration legislation, discrimination in employment, 'saturation' policing and other acts by the state.

I want to stress the point that the construction of an authoritarian state in Britain is fundamentally connected with the elaboration of the popular racism in the 1970s. Poulantzas has argued that late capitalist states have moved from the interventionist state of the post-war period to the technocratic state of today.[20] The state now not only acts to meet the needs and processes of production and reproduction but is a constituent element of these processes. There has been a rapid development of direct state control, an all-pervasive state regulation of every sphere of socio-economic life, a development in embryonic form of state authoritarianism. The state cannot ignore the need to maintain the conditions of capital accumulation; neither can it ignore for long the necessity to organize consent.

Race has increasingly become one of the means through which hegemonic relations are secured in a period of structural crisis. Race has been used to construct explanations, and therefore consent, at a time when the crisis has had to be 'managed'. Stuart Hall and others have written convincing accounts about this; how in the 1970s the British media offered a stark choice between authority and disorder, and how there were calls for immediate action.[21] By the mid-1970s it was possible to present blacks as the main danger to society and the crisis of the British way of life came to be seen everywhere – on the streets, in the family and in the schools.

There has been a direct intervention by the state into the home and school, under the guise of compensating for the inadequacies of black parents. Cultural shock, cultural conflict, generational conflict, the pathological structure of the black family – all justified increased intervention into home and school by state agencies. There is now an increasingly close link between the social services, the police and the schools for another reason: the disciplining of black youth. The construction of the 'fear' of disruption and crime by black youth is used as a justification to police them in schools.

From the above account it can be seen that policies are not

always uniform but result from a sometimes contradictory series of decisions and non-decisions taken to meet perceived or real dangers. *In school and in society, 'reform' and repression interpenetrate each other in complex, uneven and contradictory ways.* Political, legal and educational institutions are arenas of struggle. The reproduction of hegemony is never stable or guaranteed, it is constantly being reshaped and undermined. This is because wherever there is power there is resistance.

Chapter 6

White feminism, black women and schooling

The appropriation of discourses

It has been said by Michael Foucault, the French archaeologist of knowledge, that an education system is the constitution of a doctrinal group, a distribution and an appropriation of discourse, and a means of qualifying the speaking subjects. He writes;

> But we know very well that, in its distribution, in what it permits and what it prevents, it follows the lines laid down by social differences, conflicts and struggles. Every educational system is a political means of maintaining or modifying the appropriation of discourses, with the knowledge and power they bring with them.[1]

For Foucault discourses are practices that systematically form the objects of which they speak. Some of the procedures that control discourse are well known. Firstly, there is prohibition; we know very well that we are not free to speak of anything when and where we like. The second principle of exclusion is that of revision and rejection; for example, the discourse of a black person is not treated in the same way as that of a white person. Then, thirdly, there are 'societies of discourse', whose function is to preserve discourse by producing it in a restricted group.[2]

Let us consider some of these exclusions. It is now a cliché to state that the sociology of education neglected, 'could not

56

find', 'could not incorporate', or 'simply forgot' gender. Madeleine MacDonald, for example, has argued that the work of Althusser, Bowles and Gintis, and Bernstein, which focuses on social reproduction, is inadequate because it ignores the importance of the sexual division of labour within education.[3] They neglect the fact that patriarchial relationships are a central organizing principle in both the process of reproduction and within the labour process itself.

Though MacDonald has drawn our attention to the exclusion of gender by the theorists of social reproduction, her own work neglects the dimension of *race*. Her analysis contains many ethnocentric assumptions and she does not seem to be aware that black women have a very different experience of patriarchy compared with white women.

Marxist feminism and liberal feminism

Madeleine MacDonald (now Arnot) is one of a group of marxist feminists who argue that to fully comprehend class relations our understanding must be informed by a knowledge of sex/gender relations. An analysis of these relations is gradually being put together by marxist feminists such as Madeleine Arnot, Miriam David, Rosemary Deem, Angela McRobbie, Anne Marie Wolpe and others. Though not a distinct group they are all concerned with similar questions: what is the role of education in the reproduction of gender relations? Why are men and women allocated different roles in the occupational structure? How can one change gender relations in school when they are so engrained in society?

These writers have many differences with those feminists who espouse the dominant 'liberal' model. Liberal feminists (I am thinking of someone like Dale Spender) stress the idea of equality of opportunity rather than demand a fundamental change in society.[4] When these reformists write about schooling they emphasize the importance of challenging sex/gender stereotyping and the seeking of curriculum reforms. They argue, for example, that it is important for girls to take up science. But if one considers the facts that capitalist science is used to increase industrial proficiency regardless of human cost, that it is used for the purposes of militarism and social control, then the idea of 'equal opportunity' for girls to foster these becomes questionable.

Though some of the work of liberal feminists is useful, much of it, firstly, tends to see the school in isolation from its social context. Secondly, they seem to regard the state as if it was some sort of neutral adjudicator, or umpire, above 'sectional conflicts'. Thirdly, as they explain the oppression of women by patriarchy, concepts such as class and class struggle are not used. They do not consider how capital makes use of the social divisions between men and women, blacks and whites. They also neglect the influence and effects of capital on schooling.[5]

Marxist feminists tend to focus on the relationship between gender and class. Some of them suggest that the reproduction of class and gender may be *separate* processes and that both must be considered. Gender divisions are not necessarily inherent in the capitalist system but have been used by capital. In contrast to liberal feminists, marxist feminists consider schools in their historical and cultural contexts. They believe that in order to understand class and sex/gender relationships, the workplace, the school and the family should be seen as a whole. They emphasize gender differentiation within each class. Let us now consider *'the family'*.

Whilst a great deal of work has been done on the school, 'the family' has been neglected in the sociology of education. Of course, a few theorists have writen perceptively about the family. Pierre Bourdieu, for example, has described the family as a repository of 'cultural capital' which children inherit. There is a difference between the home and the school which should be noted: in the family, beliefs are inherited, whilst in school young people learn by negotiation and the creation of meaning.

Marxist feminists believe that the early years are very formative and want to focus on the family because that is where notions of gender are formed. Schools, after all, only continue the socialization process begun in the family.[6] It is not just a matter of the family existing till the child is five, and then the school taking over. The family is a set of relations interacting throughout the life of the child – an ongoing, changing process. Moreover, we should remember that schoolchildren are coping with puberty, and how persons feel about their family and class during adolescence may affect their attitudes in later life. At the present time there is a considerable outpouring of pro-family rhetoric from the political Right. The domestic role of women is being glorified and it is said that the family is sacred. But the traditional nuclear family no longer exists in Britain – there is a mismatch between the ideology of the family and how people actually live. For example, many families in Britain are now single-parent.[7] Conservative rhetoric goes hand in hand with the move towards privatization and cuts in social welfare. The Left reacts to the propaganda of the Right by loudly defending the family; it thus becomes even more pro-family than Thatcher at a time when it should be attacking Thatcherism. Increasingly it is assumed that mothers and daughters should take care of the young, the elderly and the sick, but marxists argue that the state should be responsible for the education and welfare of all people.

Criticisms of white feminism

Whilst I am most sympathetic to the marxist feminists and agree entirely with their criticisms of liberal feminists, I do have some reservations about their work. I want to argue that they lack an understanding of what 'the family' might mean to black people, and that much of white feminist theory, *liberal and marxist,* is not only irrelevant to black women but actually excludes them.

In capitalist societies the family is the site for the reproduction of labour power. There, the woman's domestic labour is essential to the rearing of future workers and the day-to-day sustenance and maintenance of the male productive worker. Marxists and feminists have been discussing for some time whether domestic labour contributes to the value of labour power and therefore indirectly to surplus value.[8] But these discussions of domestic labour, and whether its contribution is direct or indirect to surplus value, have been Eurocentric in that they are premised on the significance and meaning of domestic work for women in Western European countries only.

Black women are now beginning to question the taken-for-granted assumptions of white feminists. Hazel Carby, for example, has argued that concepts such as 'the family', 'patriarchy' and 'reproduction' are usually applied in the context of the history of white women, but when they are applied to the lives and experiences of black women, contradictions appear.[9] To cite an instance: in the analysis of white nuclear families one often reads of the role of the 'dependent' female; however, in black families there are many situations in which black women are heads of households or where, because of an economic system which structures high male unemployment, they are not financially dependent upon a black man.

Racism affects family structures in that it ensures that black men do not have the same relations to patriarchal capitalist hierarchies as white men. Black male dominance does not exist in the same form as white male dominance, as the use of the term 'sexism' implies. Systems of slavery, colonialism and *imperialism* have systematically denied positions in the white male hierarchy to black men and have used specific forms of terror to suppress them.

This, however, does not mean that the family is not a source of oppression for black women; but what is essential is an understanding of how the black family has functioned as a prime source of resistance to oppression during slavery and periods of colonialism and under the present authoritarian state.

Many white feminists work with a model of the white nuclear family in their heads, and so when black family structures differ from this they are labelled 'pathological'. In the West it is always assumed that nuclear family structures (based, of course, on some notion of romantic 'love') are more 'progressive' than black family structures. And so Asian girls and women are stereotyped as having absolutely no freedom, whereas English girls are thought to live in a liberated society. Too often concepts of historical progress are invoked by feminists to create a sliding scale of 'civilized' behaviour.

Many marxists do something similar; they view the Third World as if its pre-capitalist forms were oppressive to women, whilst capitalism is seen as the agent of amelioration and advance. Most marxists see the changes brought by imperialism to Third World societies as historically progressive. Some marxists/feminists assume that it is only through the development of a Western-style industrial capitalism and the resultant entry of black women into waged labour that the potential for the liberation of women can increase. In short, feminist theory in Britain is almost wholly Eurocentric.

Additionally, feminist theory, in concentrating only upon the isolated position of white women in the Western nuclear family structure, has neglected the very strong female support networks that exists in many black societies. Black women may lack technological aids but their shared labour, in the fields and in the market, enable them to share information and develop a sense of solidarity. Some of these strong female support networks continue in Britain amongst Afro-Caribbean and Asian communities.

There is a growing body of black feminist criticism of white feminist theory and practice for its incipient racism and lack of relevance to black women. Hazel Carby writes;

> It is not just our *herstory* before we came to Britain that has been ignored by white feminists, our experiences and struggles here have also been ignored. The struggles and experiences, because they have been structured by racism, have been different to those of white women.[10]

Many black women feel strongly that the white feminist movement has not yet recognized the fact that white women are in a power relation as oppressors of black women. Indeed, it has been said that racism in the feminist movement has excluded the participation of black women:

> White women in the British WLM are extraordinarily reluctant to see themselves in the situation of being oppressors, as they feel that this will be at the expense of concentrating upon being oppressed. Consequently the involvement of British women in imperialism and colonialism is repressed and the benefits that they – as whites – gained from the oppression of black people ignored. Forms of imperialism are simply identified as aspects of an all-embracing patriarchy rather than as sets of social

relations in which white women hold positions of power by virtue of their 'race'.[11]

Let me give a specific example. In India, during the time of British rule, the white English woman who was seen as inferior because of her sex was also seen as superior because of her 'race', even in relationship to men of another race. The benefits of a white skin did not just apply to a few memsahibs; all women in Britain benefited, in varying degrees, from the economic exploitation of the colonies.

White and black girls in school

In this section I will focus again on schooling. I will look at two studies of adolescent girls; the first is a study of white girls who stress their femininity in order to express their rejection of schooling. The second study is of black girls who place a high value on femininity *and* academic success.

A criticism that could be made of the early work of marxist feminists is that it did have some functionalist traits. Following Bowles and Gintis, it was said that schooling was 'functional for capitalism', its main aim being the reproduction of the labour force. Gradually, it has been recognized that this reproduction thesis is reductionist, lacking in mediations, and should therefore be modified. It is now generally held that the education system has a certain autonomy, and that different economic and political conditions produce different outcomes. Schooling is complex, uneven and contradictory, a site of class struggle.

In the last few years, as a reaction against the determinism of the Bowles and Gintis thesis, there has been a fashionable search for examples of resistance. Angela McRobbie, for instance, has drawn attention to the resistance of schoolgirls.[12] She has written about how many white working-class girls reject docility and stress their sexuality which is invariably defined as 'deviant'. (It has been suggested that whilst some middle-class girls adopt an anti-academic stance, many working-class girls become 'anti-school'.) By adopting an exaggerated femininity the girls prepare themselves for their future subordinate roles. There is, in addition, the ideology of romance which prepares the girls for a life of dependency. They become dual workers; after wage labour they return home to domestic labour.

Some writers have suggested that this exaggerated femininity is a form of resistance; however, I believe that it may not be oppositional at all but is an expression of gullible consumerism. In many instances 'resistance' seems to take an individualistic, private form; obviously what needs to be done is for it to be politicized and made collective.

In sociology of education most of the research has focused on males and whites.[13] When black people have been studied, they have been treated as a sexually undifferentiated group. Studies on black youth have failed to include black women, in spite of the fact that the position of young black women in waged work and unemployment is far worse than that of their white peers. However, there are exceptions – one of the few studies which investigates the specific experience of black female pupils is the research by Mary Fuller.[14] It attempts to analyse simultaneously the bearing which a pupil's sex and race might have on academic aspirations and achievements. Her work contradicts the general picture of West Indian 'low attainment' and disaffection from school. She believes that for many black girls education is a way out. Many Afro-Caribbean girls are not committed to 'good behaviour' in school, but nevertheless believe that school can offer them a great deal. They think that acquiring qualifications and getting a 'good' job will help them gain some control over their lives.

The black girls she studied were in their final year of schooling in a mixed comprehensive school. In terms of classroom behaviour they all gave the appearance of being disaffected. They displayed a nicely judged insouciance for most aspects of the good pupil role. They shared with some other pupils a view of school as being 'boring', 'trivial' and 'childish' and yet, at the same time, they had high aspirations and a high degree of academic success. Indeed, their classroom behaviour was a conscious smoke-screen to confuse others and enable the girls to retain the friendship of their peer group without giving up their aspirations.

The Afro-Caribbean girls greatly admired those people that were persistent and could demonstrate that success and femininity could be reconciled. The acquisition of academic qualifications was an integral part of their sense of control over their future in their attempt to side-step discrimination that all black people suffer. The girls' pursuit of qualifications was not some kind of individualistic self-improvement but rather a necessary strategy of survival where the poor employment prospects and low wages which black males can command make it essential even in intact families for women to contribute financially to the family income.

Mary Fuller found that for Asian girls marriage was the central fact which organized their thinking about their lives at home and their opportunities at school.[15] As a principle, and despite some worries about it in practice, the arranged marriage system was something they supported. They too were keen on gaining qualifications. By pursuing prestigious courses (science, physics) the girls thought their parents might be disinclined to interrupt academic careers with premature pressures to take up a domestic one.

Fuller argues that what makes the black women's experience unique is the addition of racism to their experience of sexism. Her analysis is based on the view that the girls experience a 'double subordination'. Black working-class people are subordinated in essentially the same way as their white counterparts, but to class subordination is added that based on race and colour. Thus differences between white and black in the working class are of degree rather than kind.

I think this is wrong. Black women's experience cannot be understood by a simple combination of sexual and racial categories. The way the gender of black women is constructed differs from the construction of white femininity because it is subject to racism. In the past the idea of double subordination was thought of in terms of a simple additive model, but recent work suggests that the interaction of double subordination may have contradictory not complementary effects.

In spite of this criticism I find Mary Fuller's research valuable for the following reasons. One, it demonstrates a need for the experience of young black women to be made visible so that the structuring of racism as it affects them, as well as their brothers, can be part of our understanding of 'black youth'. Two, it is frequently asserted that teachers' expectations serve to depress the attainment of certain groups of pupils. In this particular study the black girls' achievement was *not* related to whether teachers saw them as good or bad pupils. Three, it makes the point that it is important not to treat black people as a sexually undifferentiated entity because there are important differences in the ways females and males may manifest resistance to racism in the school context.[16]

In conclusion, let me turn to the relationship between white feminism and multiracial education. Quite a few people have written about racism and sexism as if they were the same. There are colleges that provide courses on racism and sexism and treat them as if they were similar phenomena. I have heard many feminists, amongst others, making parallels between gender and race. (Perhaps this is why some of them tend to move into MRE.) I believe this view to be false; racism and sexism are *not* similar. As soon as an historical analysis has been made, it becomes clear that the institutions which have to be analysed are different as are the forms of analysis needed.

One of the reasons why I am opposed to white feminist groups, particularly the bourgeois and reformist ones, is that their work in schools diverts and fragments political struggle within MRE. Secondly, most white women teachers know very little, on the whole, about black women's problems and so I am sceptical of the value of their contribution to anti-racist teaching. Thirdly, I am opposed to the influence of MRE because it contains a large element of feminist theory which, as I have argued in this chapter, is Eurocentric. Many of the concepts central to feminism are problematic when applied in MRE. Black women feel that it is Western women that are defining the parameters of discussion and providing the criteria of 'good practice'. Similarly, it is the metropolitan centres of the West that define the questions to be asked of other social systems and, at the same time, provide the measure against which all 'foreign' practices are gauged. It is not surprising that most of the multiracial education that goes on in schools is 'multiracial' only in name.

Chapter 7

Black youth, schooling and unemployment

Introduction: black migrant labour

In the 1950s Britain needed all the labour it could get. It should be remembered that when blacks migrated to Britain they were basically *settlers*, not migrants. This means that black workers in Britain are not like the transitory, migrant 'guest-workers' in Europe who have no right of abode in the country where they work.

The volume of migrant labour is not something to be taken as given but is created and recreated by the state. Labour power is regulated by the state through the politico-legal mechanisms of immigration legislation. The argument that immigration legislation has been used as a form of control that would ensure a labour supply best matched to the needs of capital at different times has been developed by A. Sivanandan.[1] He has argued that the legislation on immigration control culminating in the 1971 Act can be viewed as a progression towards a European migrant labour system.

There is a great deal of evidence to show that, firstly, discrimination on the basis of racism enables heightened exploitation of black 'immigrants' and thus enhances profits, and secondly, that capital has not had to bear the cost of educating and training 'immigrant' labour.[2]

In the 1970s an economic crisis developed in Western capitalist countries. Britain, like the rest of Europe, no longer needed cheap black labour. Instead of importing labour into the metropolis, capital began moving to the 'Third World' where cheap labour could be easily exploited. It has been suggested that in the Western industrial nations full employment will not occur again in this century. Perhaps the last three words should be deleted.[3]

The economic and ideological arguments

Black youth is disproportionately represented in the unemployment figures. This is a brutal fact because occupation, or the lack of it, is a basic determinant of class position; it crucially affects every aspect of our lives. The unemployment rate among West Indian school leavers is four times as high as the national average.[4] What is the reason for this?

There are some 'liberal' writers who argue that the phenomenon of black unemployment cannot be explained by economic factors alone. Their research usually stresses racial discrimination and racial disadvantage. John Rex's work, for example, focuses on the stratified nature of the 'host community' (doesn't a 'host' imply a 'guest'?), highlighting the fact that the immigrant is likely to enter a highly unequal society at its most disadvantageous point.[5] An important feature of his research is his recognition of the relevance of colonialism for an understanding of the current racial situation in Britain. According to Rex, certain immigrant groups have particular problems which arise, firstly, because the indigenous population regard ex-colonial immigrants in terms of negative stereotypes (such as 'savages' or terrorists); and secondly, because such immigrants are forced to live in deprived inner-urban areas. Taking together the two facts of the emergence of relatively deprived industrial roles and of deprived neighbourhoods, one can see that the immigrant worker is likely to be categorized as belonging to a separate group, and in times of crises made a scapegoat. Rex's work, though it usefully concentrates on the effects of colonialism, neglects consideration of the economic dimension. I would want to argue that even if all racial discrimination were removed, exploitation of black *workers* would still continue.

Let us now turn to look at the tendencies within capitalism

that lead to the development of a deskilled or mainly unemployed proletariat. Many economists, such as Ernest Mandel, have pointed out that one of the most important developments that has occurred since the Second World War is the change in the labour process.[6] The scientific-technological revolution ensures increasing productivity by employing a diminishing workforce. There is a general tendency towards increasing unemployment (which is sometimes balanced in particular economies by displacing the problem elsewhere). Braverman, amongst others, has stressed the fact that most people in capitalism have work that is monotonous and repetitive and requires only a minimal level of training.[7] These workers are, therefore, easily substituted and have little bargaining power in times of recession.

Though economic arguments can help to explain the causes of unemployment they do not explain why black youth is disproportionately represented in the unemployment figures.[8] Besides economic arguments we must therefore use arguments drawn from the theory of ideology.

I have already mentioned the point that ideology is not mere illusion or misconception of the real. Ideas are real and not 'ideal' because they are always inscribed in social practices and are expressed in objective social forms; as such they have definite effects.[9] In other words, ideology first works itself out in practices, and therefore we must analyse the practices and not the beliefs that people express. The congregation of black people in certain parts of cities, their attendance at certain inner-city schools, their unemployment – all these are expressions of racist, material *practices*. Material practices ensure that racism structures the everyday life of black people.

Another important point is that it is through ideology that people live their lives, imagining that their choices determine what they do. People do not fully understand the conditions in which they live; knowledge of the conditions is not available to experience, but is acquired through theoretical understanding of the inner workings of the structure. Now, though racist beliefs are based on 'imaginary' perceptions of black people, the material conditions that produce them are real enough. Black people provide an obvious immediate explanation for the problems of white people. In a period of economic crisis any visible outgroup in competition for scarce resources is an easy target for scapegoating.

At the present time, when more blacks (proportionately) are suffering from unemployment than other groups, the discourse of racism is being linked with the discourse of nationalism: 'Our cities are so overcrowded. . . . Why has s/he got a job while I'm unemployed? Why don't they go back home? I am sure they would be happy and we would be happier as well.' Such racist beliefs are an attempt to understand and explain daily experience but, of course, the real reasons for the capitalist crisis are abstract and these socio-economic processes cannot be grasped in terms of daily experience. Elements of 'common sense' are being taken up and systematically reorganized in order to construct more coherent, more comprehensive racist ideologies. These ideologies are now being adopted and legitimated by the state.

Schooling for unemployment

The story we are usually told is that the immigrant settlers that came to Britain were passive. This is just not true. They were politically aware, but as the conditions in which they had to live were very tough most of their energy went into coping with these poor conditions. They hoped that their life would improve and that things would be better for their children. But now these children have grown up, conditions of capital accumulation have changed in Britain and full employment policies have been abandoned by successive governments. The position of the second generation has not only failed to improve, relative to their parents' generation, but has been characterized by an increasing shift from the labour force to the industrial reserve army (the unemployed). Their labour power is no longer needed. So Britain, caught in the heritage of her colonial past, is now faced with a population of young black Britons alienated by racism and disillusioned by perpetual unemployment.

What are the effects of the high level of youth unemployment on schools? It is difficult to be precise because little research has been done on this topic. I have spoken to parents who are very worried about the situation; they are taking a great deal of interest in the education of their children and are becoming more involved in their children's choice of examination subjects. Many young people who cannot get jobs are staying on in the sixth form and in some schools there is an increased demand for courses such as bookkeeping, crafts, computer studies and communication skills, which have a greater vocational component. It seems that whilst some pupils in schools are working harder, others think, 'As we have no chance of getting a job, what is the point of studying?'

What I find interesting is that in Britain problems of school achievement appear to take precedence over policies of positive discrimination in employment. In the field of *education* there appears to be an enthusiasm to compensate for the deficiences of the groups identified as requiring attention. This is called negative compensation. In *employment* there is a lack of willingness to admit the need for special provision for these groups. This could be called positive non-discrimination. It can be concluded that there is intervention in some fields and its studious avoidance in others.[10]

Just over half a million young people left school in 1983/4, and embarked on a desperate search for work. Some of them accepted jobs they would hitherto have regarded as below their competence level; in other words, there is a vocational shift downmarket. 'Credential inflation' occurs. Employers are demanding higher social and academic qualifications for increasingly deskilled jobs. This produces a concertina effect on the opportunity structure for school leavers; 'A' levels are required for jobs which previously needed 'O' levels and so on down the line. Employers also prefer mature, experienced women as (part-time) workers to school leavers.

School leavers and state intervention

The disproportionate concentration of potentially militant young blacks among the unskilled and the unemployed is not only a focus of disquiet among the black community, but also presents a problem for the state. During the present crisis new forms of state intervention have been created and used. The whole educational system is being changed; a new discourse is being constructed.

In this process blacks, and the young working class, are being defined as being 'deficient', lacking in literacy, numeracy and other skills. The inadequacies of school leavers are being continually stressed by right-wing educationalists, industrialists and others who have access to the media. Industrialists have argued that there is a 'mismatch' between what the schools teach their pupils and the 'needs' of industry. And so the impression has been created that the problem is not the capitalist mode of production but the inadequacy of young people. Through this ideology the young are being blamed for their unemployment.

Many reasons are given for this 'inadequacy'. It is said that poor attitudes to work stem from progressive teaching methods, defects in the comprehensive school system, or the incompetence of (badly trained) teachers. But one fact is hardly mentioned: the point that youth unemployment is not accidental. Development in science and technology and changes in the labour process mean that there are no jobs for young people; casual and unskilled manual work has disappeared. In the present set-up the capitalist labour process cannot be altered and so an attempt is being made to re-process the thoughts and attitudes of young people.

One of the key institutions in the restructuring process is the Manpower Services Commission (MSC). Around 1976 unemployment was seen as temporary and a cyclical phenomenon, but now it is seen as a permanent feature and the MSC has become very active and powerful. It keeps nearly one million people off the unemployment statistics. (In some regions – there are amazing regional disparities in unemployment in Britain – the MSC is the only source of 'work' for young people.)

The select Committee on Race Relations 1975–6 noted the reluctance of young West Indians to use the services of the MSC and the Careers Service because of what was termed 'alienation'. Throughout MSC documents 'alienation', work-refusal and non-registration of black youth are described as an actual and potential threat to the social fabric.

71

Criticisms of the youth training schemes

What criticisms can be made of the training schemes organized by the MSC, on behalf of the government, for the black and white working class? The training given on these schemes is based on a notion of 'core' skills that, once developed, can be adapted across a wide range of occupations. The emphasis is on the transferability of those basic skills. Some trade unionists see this non-specific training in terms of the 'deskilling' that has taken place over the last ten years in the shift from manual and craft industries towards the automated processes that employers are now using.

There is an attempt to change the status of young workers or apprentices to 'trainees' (a term which will eventually replace apprentices). The schemes represent a further attempt to keep down wage levels for the young. Moreover, the schemes are often abused by sponsors and employers, and in many cases trainees, who are cheap labour, take the place of people who could be employed. In a period of recession employers have considerable power, and some of them exploit young people, making them do dangerous work. Many deaths have taken place.[11]

It is obvious that one of the main aims of the government is to get young people away from the streets and on to MSC courses. The government can then distract attention from the structural problems of capitalism and blame the young for their unemployment because of 'deficiencies' in their schooling. This justifies the various training schemes whose main function is to socialize and incorporate the young unemployed into the discipline of work, even if there are no real jobs available. At the same time, the government can say, 'Look what we are doing. The unemployment statistics have stopped rising. See how constructive we are!'

It should be noted that all the schemes of the MSC have a 'hidden curriculum' which attempts to influence the beliefs of young people. I believe that racial and sexual divisions are being reproduced by the MSC. The training programmes offer nothing concrete to offset the disadvantage of female and black workers in the labour market, despite official equal opportunity policies. I also think that through the social policies of the MSC the traditional distinction between 'education' and 'training' has become blurred and redefined.[12] Training schemes are now being introduced into schools, coupled with what is called 'social education'. The young are seen to have certain 'needs' and they are to be provided for by new schemes. As for the MSC, it admits that its new schemes have nothing to do with job creation – they are basically to do with work socialization. It should also be said that because of the shift in attention to the problems of the 16–19 age range many reforms urgently needed elsewhere in the educational system (the reduction of class size in comprehensive schools, for example) are not being carried out.

In my view there has been a bland consensus amongst the political parties about youth unemployment. The unions have become more and more involved with capitalist institutions (like the Confederation of British Industry) and the state. As a result of this corporatist policy new strategies are being used to control the young working-class unemployed between school and wage labour. And so we have moved from the ideological notion of a liberal 'education' towards an acceptance of education *and* training. In the near future the 'training' element will increase. From a situation in which agencies have an advising, guiding role we are gradually moving towards a time when they will use compulsion.

Now, my main concern about these schemes is that *they are only for blacks and working-class youth.* Why should this be so? Why is it that privileged groups in our society receive a theoretical/abstract education to a high level which is then followed by training and work experience, whilst the mass of school leavers, ejected after only a low level of education, are given a narrow, *manual* training?

The separation of mental and manual labour

I want to argue that the explanation for the education/training split is related to the main role of the educational system, particularly the school, which is to reproduce and legitimate the separation of mental and manual labour. What has happened in capitalism is that the mental labour necessary to production, formerly united with manual labour in the production process, has become the prerogative of capital and separate from the manual tasks of execution. It is this appropriation of the knowledge necessary to production by the capitalist class that characterizes and gives rise to the hierarchical division between mental and manual labour. In all areas of social and economic life we see that those who conceptualize, control, plan and manage are in authoritarian positions over those who merely execute tasks.[13]

The school reproduces the hierarchial separation of mental and manual labour through two related features: the separation between the school and production, and the qualification of mental labour and the disqualification of manual labour by the school itself. Let us look at the formal separation that exists between the school and production. This separation between school and work is itself based on the separation of the direct producer from the means of production. Schools are institutionally separated from factories and other work sites. This separation gives rise to the relative autonomy of the school and allows it to be presented as an 'independent', neutral, apolitical institution which separates the learning processes of the adult and the child.

The separation of school and production has many other effects. It ensures that all school knowledge is formulated and taught in the framework of imaginary, not real, problems, and this reduces the possibility of a critical assessment of that knowledge. The separation of schooling from everyday experience also has the effect that for manual labour, both during and after school, knowledge is seen as 'useless' abstract knowledge. For manual labour school knowledge becomes a thing of childhood, an abstraction to be escaped from.

School, then, for many working-class and black youngsters is associated with mental labour, abstraction and imposition. However, as Paul Willis has shown, in rejecting mental labour the counter-school culture does not in fact challenge it, but merely confirms itself as manual labour.[14] Individual resistance to schooling in the school itself affirms manual labour in opposition to mental labour. And so the reproduction of the mental/manual division continues unchallenged.

By excluding pupils from the economic and political

struggles in society the school ensures an antiseptic education which accepts capitalist relations of production as a given, a schooling for the status quo. To recapitulate: the fact that learning takes place in institutions divorced from daily life and experience serves to reproduce and legitimize the division between mental and manual labour. This separation reflects the division between culture and production, theory and practice.

There is an advantage in seeing capitalist education in this way, namely that the reproduction of the mental/manual split by and through the school leaves space for different degrees of correspondence/non-correspondence between schooling and the capitalist economy.[15] It allows for the relative autonomy of education, the wide variety of social relations, curricular organization and content found in schools. In other words, the school system is not just a mirror-image of social relations of the workplace.[16] Nor does schooling have to respond in any simple, direct way to economic demands. All kinds of things can and do happen in school without necessarily challenging the school's role in reproducing the division between mental and manual labour.

Some people may think that this thesis is not relevant because work experience schemes are being fostered by the government and that attempts are being made to relate schools and colleges with industry. But, as I have already suggested, youth training schemes focus primarily on narrowly defined technical skills which will enable manual workers to execute the labour process more efficiently. All these schemes rigidly reinforce the mental/manual division. This is not to deny that the government finds them useful for many other reasons too. In the last few years there have been violent risings in London and Liverpool, Bristol and Manchester, in which black and white youth have protested together. Youth training schemes are not only a way of removing school leavers from the dole queue and deregistering them from the unemployment statistics; they are also means of social control, attempts to discipline working-class youth.

Youth unemployment and cultural change: some speculations

So far in this chapter I have outlined some of the massive changes that have taken place in Britain during the last few years. Because of the crisis in capitalism there is a fundamentally *new* state of affairs. In this section, therefore, I will draw to your attention some of the cultural changes that are taking place now.

Until recently young people had an unproblematic transition from schooling to employment; one day they were in school, the next day they were at work. The 'wage' was very important for working-class youth as it meant that one could stop being dependent on one's parents and set up a home of one's own. The pain of work was balanced by the pleasure of consumership and there was a chance to exercise some consumer power in the High Street. But all this is now changing.

As we have seen, the state is taking an active interest in this area partly because working-class youth is becoming increasingly restive. On the one hand, the MSC is extending its role and power and yet, at the same time, another ideological and contradictory response by the state is to call unemployment 'leisure'. How are the young responding to this new social condition? Whilst adults have some educational resources because they have had experience of work and their identities are formed, the young unemployed have not had work experience. An extraordinarily high percentage of the young unemployed do not go to any youth clubs, join political parties, or take part in any organized activity. Many young wageless people are isolated in their homes, lonely and in despair.

For most people cultural knowledge comes from the experience of work, of being in a collective work group. People gain their identity from work. It is the main way working-class people gain knowledge about politics. In the labour process workers are always involved in two courses of action: the humanizing of production and the continual struggle to control the work process. It is this struggle that provides an understanding of how capitalism operates. Isn't it possible that young people who no longer have the experience of contestation will become de-politicized?

It has been suggested by Paul Willis that there may be a connection between manual labour and a certain kind of masculinity.[17] For the man in work respect is given not for what he is, but for what he knows, what he makes. If certain patriarchal attitudes develop through manual labour, then it may well be that the loss of work will have damaging effects on gender identity. Unemployed men no longer have the security of a certain sort of dignity. As a consequence there may be an increase of aggression amongst groups of young males. But this is only a speculation; it is possible that young working-class men may become more gentle and sensitive.

Besides youth unemployment, the state is also intervening in the family. The nuclear family is under terrible strain as the state tries to persuade women to stay at home to look after the young, the ill and the old. Another remarkable social trend is the large number of young unmarried women who are becoming mothers. For those 'solo' parents there is no access to consumerism. In spite of material hardship these young women see motherhood as a way of being creative and fulfilling onself.

Whilst adults in employment are celebrating consumerism, unemployed young people have lost their consumer power. In the past, people worked and suffered to buy commodities that made them fit and well enough to make them want to work again to buy some more commodities. This cycle is now broken. Nevertheless, popular culture is based more and more on consumption. Consumerism says that it is good to buy things, but if the access to commodities is broken, then is it possible that a pathological attitude to things may develop? The working class suffer in making things, and so it could be said that they are inoculated against consumerism. But what will be the attitude of the young towards commodities if they have no experience of the hard work involved in making things on the factory floor? Could the young unemployed come to regard commodities as if they were made by magic?

There is, of course, another possibility: the media and the whole culture are telling us all the time that things are good, but if there is no money, why not get them by theft? There are some socialists who have glorified crime and have seen it as a sort of resistance. But not all crime is resistance, some crime is crime. Is it possible for the wageless to reject consumerism altogether? Could a new form of socialization, not based on work or consumerism, come about?

In this new situation we have to face some difficult questions: what does the 'wage' mean and what should be done about wagelessness? (Here our definition of the wage should not be economistic or our solutions, too, will be economistic.) We should demand youth employment but we must recognize that full employment in the future is highly unlikely under capitalism. Moreover, we should not forget the drudgery and toil of many jobs, the inadequacy of the reward and the triviality of the products. Many blacks are already refusing to accept passively the consequences of the economic crisis and the political crisis that flows from it. This is part of a renewed criticism of a society that measures worth by the work that you do and not by the sort of person you are.

The unity of learning and labour

One of the main points that I have been trying to stress in this book is that capital constantly struggles to ensure that the knowledge which gives access to power remains in its own hands. The knowledge which is involved in positions of control in production and society is effectively taught only to a few in institutions of higher education. Agents of mental labour, because of their access to specialized forms of knowledge, share in the rewards of capital by possessing some degree of autonomy in their own work situation and/or themselves being involved in the planning, conception, management and control of production processes which are executed by other, manual workers. These agents form the new middle class.

If the school in capitalism, as I have suggested, is intrinsically an anti-working-class institution which reinforces and reproduces the separation of the working class from the means of production, what should be done? I want to argue that one crucial change required is that schools should be integrated with production and the wider society. This is not a new idea; there have been attempts at such an integration in many countries at different times.

In England, for example, the working class in the nineteenth century attempted to integrate its own independent educational forms with its own needs. There was an attempt to link education with the daily lives of the working class, to unify theory and practice. Richard Johnson has documented how the provision of universal state education was, in part, a way of undermining and destroying this oppositional working-class education:

> The consequences of this adaptation were immense: it involved, for instance, accepting, in a very sharp form, the child-adult divide, the tendency to equate education with school, the depoliticization of educational content, and the professionalization of teaching. In all these ways the state as educator was by no means a neutral apparatus.[18]

Marx, influenced by the social experiments of Robert Owen in New Lanarkshire, believed that the true humanity of people was related to work (work is alienating only in a capitalist society), and that in a socialist society education must be combined with work. These ideas were taken up by the Bolsheviks in the Soviet Union, where an attempt was made to provide a socialist education.

After the Russian Revolution in 1917 there were many conflicting ideas about the best way the new society could integrate work and learning. Were the activities to be combined in the same place or in two different institutions? Was learning to be introduced into labour or should labour be introduced into the school?

There were many exciting experiments during the early years of the revolution but by the 1930s the Party had intervened with a hard line and the many progressive experiments were brought to an end. Education was too important to be left to the educators. School councils became moribund, the authority of schoolteachers was reinstated, school uniform and homework returned. The Soviet educational system became highly (verbal and) formal. The polytechnical idea was replaced by the monotechnic, and education came to be redefined as *the preparation* for labour.

The contradictions that existed in the early years of the Soviet state between education and the economy still exist in many less developed countries today. Education should emphasize the development of the social individual, the democratic, thinking individual who needs a wide general knowledge, but the economy (especially in the 'Third World') demands skilled labour, and so there is a tendency for specialization to begin earlier and earlier.

To conclude this chapter, let me recapitulate the key points. It has been argued that capitalist society controls us by the knowledge it teaches us, since it does not teach us what we need to know to control and shape society. Schools tend to reproduce and legitimize the division between mental and manual labour. That is why learning takes place in institutions divorced from daily life and experience. Though government training schemes want school and work to be brought together, they want this only in so far as they rigidly *reinforce* the hierarchial mental/manual division.

I have suggested that schools should be united with production and the wider society, and I cited the experiments of the working class in nineteenth-century England and the Bolsheviks in Russia as examples. Though it may appear that both the Left and the Right want to bring learning and labour together, it is vital that the difference between the two positions be clearly recognized. Whilst the Right defines these schemes in terms of a limiting and restrictive training for manual labour, socialists must struggle for an education and society based on the dialectical *unity* of mental and manual labour.

Chapter 8

Hegemony, race and class

Introduction

I begin this chapter by briefly outlining Gramsci's concept of hegemony, his views on teachers and intellectuals, and the role of popular struggles that express the deepest needs of all people. I then go on to introduce the work of two contemporary 'discourse' theorists, Ernesto Laclau and Chantal Mouffe, who, greatly influenced by Gramsci's thought, have made an important advance in the study of hegemony. I focus particularly on Laclau's work on fascism because it is important for us to understand how that movement utilized certain ideologies, such as racism and nationalism, for the purpose of mass mobilization. There is then a discussion of the relationship between capitalism, race and class: should black people subsume the race struggle to the class struggle, or should the struggle of black people be separate and autonomous? The final section relates class and race to the ideological battle being fought out in schools over the role of 'ethnicity' and 'cultural pluralism' in multiracial education.

Hegemony

Gramsci shares with Lenin and Trotsky the distinction of being one of the three most significant and influential marxist theorists of the imperial epoch as well as being directly active in revolutionary communist politics. But, whereas the views of Lenin and Trotsky were decisively shaped by the revolutionary process in backward Russia, Gramsci was concerned above all with the conditions for a successful revolution in more advanced capitalist societies.

In Gramsci's work there is a rejection of all forms of economism. He emphasizes that one cannot reduce questions of political practice to those concerned with the mode of production. Although economic crisis may weaken the state, they cannot in themselves produce great historical events. A revolutionary movement, therefore, cannot restrict itself to economic struggles but must combine them with political and ideological struggles.

Gramsci argued that the state is an organization of class domination which operates through a variable combination of coercion and consent. He identified two modes of class domination: force, the use of coercive apparatus to bring about conformity and compliance, and hegemony. Hegemony involves the successful mobilization and reproduction of the 'active consent' of dominated groups by the ruling class through the exercise of intellectual, moral and political leadership. Hegemony is an organizing principle or combination of world views diffused by agencies of ideological control – it socializes people in every area of daily life.[1] It is not a matter of indoctrination or 'false consciousness'. It is not constructed by the coercion of one class; it is created with the *consent* of other groups. The maintenance of hegemony involves taking systematic account of popular interests and the making of compromises (on secondary issues) to maintain support. There are two types of hegemony: passive hegemony works by absorbing and thus neutralizing other movements; expansive hegemony works by actually acceding to their demands.[2] But we must remember that in some societies hegemony is never really achieved and that in others it cannot be constituted.

The practice of hegemony is concentrated in the sphere of *civil society* or so-called 'private' organizations such as the church, trade unions, political parties, the mass media, schools, and in the activities of intellectuals. Gramsci suggested that the institutions of civil society were weak in the East, the Russia of 1917, but in the advanced capitalist systems of the West the strength of hegemonic apparatuses is very strong. Whilst the Tsarist state could be smashed largely through a quick 'war of manoeuvre' organized by the Bolshevik party, a successful revolution in the West pre-supposes a long 'war of position' to alter the relations of forces and prepare for a transition to socialism.[3]

Teachers, intellectuals and ideology

Gramsci believed that teachers and intellectuals have a key role in the preparation for socialism because their function is to educate the people. This view was based on his insightful analysis of the division of mental and manual labour in capitalist society.

He held that manual labour estranges working-class people from mental labour in two senses. Firstly, exclusion from paid mental labour limits the ability of workers to accustom themselves to the demands of mental activity in any sustained way. Everybody thinks, but the fact that most workers are not paid to do so narrows their intellectual needs.

The second sense in which workers are alienated from mental activity lies in their ignorance of the ways in which knowledge is acquired in a scholarly or academic sense. In the absence of extra-work cultural activity, or access to mental labour processes at work, how are workers to know about the nature of intellectual labour? Gramsci argued that, if people do not fully understand that intellectual skills are acquired through labour, they will believe that either learning is a matter of a 'trick' of which they are ignorant or of an innate quality which they do not possess. The historical separation of mental and manual labour in capitalist society is submerged beneath a popular ideology in which it seems right that some *think* and and others *do*. This naturalization is an important factor in the 'consent' of the masses to their own subordinate position.

This is why Gramsci wanted to *demystify the procedures of study;* in his view, education was an intervention in the social and natural world. Though he held the view that children are not passive, he believed that studying did not come easily to them. The habit of studying is only acquired through much effort, through an apprenticeship of hard work and training.[4]

In Gramsci's view, teachers were the human link between the masses and the state. As the division of labour increased, knowledge became more specialized and in this process some people had become 'intellectuals'. He said that everyone was an intellectual but that some people had the job, the function of an intellectual. He went on to make another distinction: traditional intellectuals are linked to previous modes of production and organic intellectuals are linked to one of the two fundamental classes. Intellectuals – and this includes teachers – are important because they elaborate and spread ideologies to the masses.

For Gramsci the needs of the masses were primary; *they* defined the problems. Nevertheless, he was critical of folklore, the superstitious elements within common sense.

Common sense, though based on experience, was limited. It was simple, fragmentary, contradictory; unlike 'good sense', it was not worked out critically or systematically. He argued that there was a need for a new type of intellectual, for persons who made an already existing activity coherent, critical and systematic. 'Common sense' should be transformed into 'good sense', but this can only be done by people who have relevant skills and who have an 'organic' relationship with the masses. Gramsci argued that intellectuals 'know' but do not feel while workers feel but do not 'know'; hence the need for a synthesis of intellectual knowledge and working-class experience for the production of a socialist culture.

It should be noted that in Gramsci's work there are parallels between a series of dominant-subordinate terms: good sense – common sense, philosophy – folklore, high culture – popular culture, intellectuals – people, party – masses. The point in each case is not to impose the former on the latter but to construct an educative alliance between them. Every relationship of hegemony is necessarily an educational relationship.[5]

Gramsci believed that superstructural phenomena such as beliefs and myths, and institutions such as media and law, function on a mass level to perpetuate existing order. He

84

held that ideological struggle was of great importance because class domination is exercised as much through popular 'consensus' as through force. We must see Gramsci's political thinking in the context of a period when imperialism was beginning to organize external markets and the state was extending into civil society. The state was beginning to manage some tasks that were previously private; education, for example, was shifting from the private to the public domain, from the family circle to the state school. All these moves were a part of the strategy of the bourgeoisie to incorporate the working class.

Gramsci, therefore, held that the main task of organic intellectuals in the socialist movement is to create a counter-hegemony to break the ideological bond between the ruling class and the rest of the population. Revolutionary potential arises at moments of crisis of ideological hegemony. Ideology is a battlefield on which there is a continuous struggle between two hegemonic principles: 'To the extent that ideologies are historically necessary they have a validity which is "psychological"; they "organise" human masses and create a terrain on which men move, acquire consciousness of their position, struggle, etc.'[6] For Gramsci, then, ideology is not based on the truth/falsity distinction. Ideology is for binding people together in order to motivate them politically. The function of ideology is to form a new collective will. According to this view, politics is not about domination but the creation of a new collective consciousness, a new culture.

As no aspect of bourgeois society is outside the class struggle or irrelevant to socialist politics, he called for the building of a mass party rooted in everyday social reality, a party built on particular, embryonic, popular struggles. He argued that there was a need to build 'national-popular' and 'popular-democratic' alliances or blocs that transcend a class base but express contemporary struggles.[7]

For revolution to become a truly popular phenomenon, it would have to speak to the customs, needs and aspirations of all the people. Revolution must transform not simply the economy but also what he called the 'ensemble of relations' – not only the economic but also ideology, politics and culture.

Gramsci's theoretical contribution

An important advance in the study of hegemony has been made by Ernesto Laclau and Chantal Mouffe. They insist that politics – the struggle to achieve class hegemony – is largely to do with the arrangement, the 'articulation' of different discourses. Their 'discourse theory' is based on an interpretation, a particular reading of Gramsci's work. They make three main points. Firstly, Gramsci rejects the idea that political forces are essentially class forces and suggests instead that political forces are constituted as interclass collective wills in and through ideological struggle.[8]

Secondly, Gramsci rejects the view that there are pure class ideologies corresponding in a paradigmatic manner to different classes. Hegemony is not achieved through the imposition of one paradigmatic class ideology on other classes – it involves the disarticulation and the rearticulation of different elements from different ideological discourses.

Thirdly, Gramsci insists that there are important ideological elements which have no necessary class connotations and belong to the field of the 'national-popular'. The two fundamental classes compete to articulate 'national-popular' elements into their own class discourse. These three theoretical points will now be elaborated.

Ideological struggle and discourse

In a famous paper Laclau writes that many studies of fascism have tended to eliminate the complex accumulation of contradictions constitutive of fascism and that, too often, fascism has been seen as the pure and simple expression of a direct dictatorship of monopoly capital over the rest of society.[9] Most writers have tended to undervalue the relative autonomy of the fascist state and the mass mobilization which preceded its coming to power. In other words, they have put the authoritarian character of fascism above its character as a mass regime.

Laclau begins by criticizing Poulantzas for holding the view that social classes have 'pure', 'necessary', or 'paradigmatic' ideologies (marxist leninism is the ideology of the working class, liberalism is the ideology of the bourgeoisie, etc.). He convincingly shows that none of the elements that Poulantzas supposes to be characteristic of the ideology of any one class is such if considered in isolation. To give just another example: liberalism, which Poulantzas considers an ideological element of the bourgeoisie during the stage of competitive capitalism, was in Latin America the characteristic ideology of the feudal landowners. In short, ideological 'elements' taken in isolation have no necessary class connotation, and this connotation is only the result of the articulation of those elements in a concrete ideological discourse.[10]

Laclau states that the function of all ideology is to constitute individuals as subjects. Individuals, who are bearers of structures, are transformed by ideology into subjects. The argument is that not every contradiction is a class contradiction and that *'the people'* form an objective determination which is different from the class determination. Every class struggles at the ideological level simultaneously as class *and* as the people, or rather, tries to give coherence to its ideological discourse by presenting its class objectives as the consummation of popular objectives.

There is the 'people'/power block contradiction, and the political struggle of the working class must tend to realize a total identity between popular struggle and socialist struggle. At the same time the bourgeoisie tends to maintain the separation between the two, so that the working class may be politically neutralized. This is called 'transformism' – the political neutralization of possible opposition from new social groups by co-option of their representative political organizations into the power bloc.

Laclau points out that at the time of the rise of nazism, Leon Trotsky saw only two possibilities: either there was class ideology in all its purity or there was the dissolution of the proletariat in 'the people'. Trotsky is typical of many on the Left who believe that nationalism is an 'element' of bourgeois ideology and, as such, is not susceptible to transformation in a socialist direction. Poulantzas also tends to consider any kind of nationalist agitation as a concession to the adversary.

Against this view Laclau argues that it was the abandonment

87

of the arena of popular-democratic struggle by socialist parties that left the way open for fascism. He insists that the class character of an ideology is given not by its content but by its *form*. Nationalism considered in itself has no class connotation. The latter only derives from its specific articulation with other ideological elements. A feudal class, for example, can link nationalism to the maintenance of a hierarchial system of a traditional type (Bismarck's Germany). A bourgeois class may link nationalism to the development of a centralized nation state and at the same time appeal to national unity as a means of neutralizing class conflicts (France). Finally, a communist movement can denounce the betrayal by capitalist classes of a nationalist cause and articulate nationalism and socialism in a single ideological discourse (Mao's China). In ideological struggle, then, each class presents itself as the authentic representative of 'the people' and of 'the national interest'.[12]

The ideology of the dominant class, precisely because it is dominant, constitutes not only the members of that class but also members of the dominated classes. There is a partial absorption and neutralization of those ideological contents through which resistance to the domination of the former is expressed. The characteristic method of securing this objective is *to eliminate antagonism and transform it into a simple difference*. A class is hegemonic not so much to the extent that it is able to impose a uniform conception of the world on the rest of society, but to the extent that it can articulate different visions of the world in such a way that their potential antagonism is neutralized.

The main task, then, is the disarticulation of bourgeois ideology and the rearticulation of its democratic elements to working-class ideology. The struggle of the working class for its hegemony is an effort to achieve the maximum possible fusion between popular-democratic ideology and socialist ideology. Laclau concludes that there is no socialism without populism, and that the highest forms of populism can only be socialist.[13] Socialist hegemony does not mean the pure and simple destruction of the previous society, but the absorption of its elements into a new articulation. It is only when socialism has developed this articulating capacity that it comes to be hegemonic.

Some comments on Laclau and Mouffe

Before I make some criticisms of the general theory of hegemony that Laclau and Mouffe are developing, let me summarize the key points. In their work the discursive is considered to be co-extensive with the social and all social relations are thought of as constituted in and through discourse. This means that they reject orthodox marxist views of 'base-superstructure' relations in which the so-called material base is seen as extra-discursive and the superstructure alone treated as discursive. One implication of this view is that the unity of the social formation depends on the contingent articulation of discursive practices.

Moreover, one can no longer privilege class subjects over popular-democratic forces nor treat class struggle as necessarily more influential than popular-democratic struggles. Class and non-class subjects are also constituted in and through discourse. It seems that the class struggle is first of all a struggle about the constitution of class subjects before it is a struggle between class subjects. And so the struggle for hegemony is reinterpreted in terms of intervention to articulate different discursive elements. Thus ideas such as the 'nation', the 'people' and the 'family' acquire different connotations according to their articulation with other elements to form a specific discourse.

What criticisms can be made of the work of Laclau and Mouffe? They believe that society is an ensemble of discursive practices: 'The discursive is the ensemble of the phenomena in and through which social production of meaning takes place.'[14] The discursive, then, is not a level, it is co-extensive with the social. But if politics is purely discursive and is not in some way about 'truth', why disarticulate the elements on behalf of socialism rather than fascism? Their work suggests that all discourses are of equal weight, but I would argue that there are differences between them in terms of weight, pressure and urgency.

Laclau and Mouffe emphasize articulation-disarticulation within discourse, but in their form of analysis it is difficult to conceptualize domination. This is partly because there is an element of idealism in their work that derives from Saussure's view of language which stressed that the meaning of a concept derives only from its relationship with other concepts – its difference. In Saussure the signified refers not to the real object, the referent, but to the concept of it. Now, I know that Laclau and Mouffe are stressing the point that one can only say anything about the real through language, but sometimes they seem to be stating that language is the only reality. There is a tendency, in other words, to collapse all practices into one discursive practice.

If all the various 'levels' or 'regions' of a social formation are constituted in and through discourse and are liable to transformation through forces which are likewise constituted, we must replace the notion of the causal primacy of the economy with a 'primacy of the political' or, more accurately, a 'primacy of the discursive'. Laclau and Mouffe stress the discursive to such an extent that they are logocentric; this textual reductionism means that they exclude the extra-discursive.[15]

To put it simply, their focus on political, intellectual and moral leadership has led to a neglect of economic contradictions and constraints. Moreover, because Laclau and Mouffe focus upon ideological discourse they exclude consideration of the administrative, economic, legal and military aspects of society. They ignore how hegemonic projects are often promoted by material inducements and bodily repression. Furthermore, we still need to explore the social conditions that determine the openness of subjects to specific projects and/or make them 'available' for mobilization.

In spite of these doubts and reservations I believe that the Left should take 'discourse analysis' seriously – it is not enough to label such work as revisionist because it challenges some orthodox marxist beliefs. Laclau and Mouffe, for example, see class formation as an effect of heterogeneous struggles premised on different communalities – linguistic, sexual, regional, ecological and racial. What I find most valuable in Laclau and Mouffe is their insistence that 'ideological struggle . . . consists of a process of disarticulation-rearticulation of given ideological elements in a struggle between two hegemonic principles to appropriate these elements, it does not consist of the confrontation of two already elaborated closed views'.[16]

Race and nation

Now, it could be said that the popular discourse of 'the nation' and 'the people' operates across the formal lines of class and has been constructed against blacks. There is a sense in which 'the British Nation' does not include black people. As the Left has often tended to stress internationalism it has never been able to deal with the discourse of nationalism adequately. Many black people in Britain, for example, feel nervous when whites parade with the national flag. For the National Front and other right-wing political groups the Union Jack has become a sign with the meaning 'We are British' — a deliberate and explicit exclusion of blacks. I want to argue that what is required is a change whereby some of the elements in this nationalist discourse are disarticulated and rearticulated in a popular, socialist ideology that integrates the discourses of class, race and nation: 'We are socialist, black *and* British.'

The blacks are only one of the new social groups that have begun to make themselves felt since the 1970s; there are also ecological, regional, youth, peace and women's movements. These protest movements are changing our conceptions not only of politics but of forms of struggle. One implication of the argument that the Left should work with the blacks and other emergent political groups is that there should be a people's party which recognizes that a Left populist democratic struggle contains many new groups and movements.

Race and class

For black people racism is an everyday occurrence that is not easy to shrug off. They feel resentful of the way that they have been used in times of labour shortage and then discarded when no longer needed. If working-class racism in the inner city is grounded in the daily experience and the material conditions of working-class life, then we can see that appeals to moral principles, 'cultural understanding' or psychological approaches are unlikely to be successful. The solution has to be political.

This brings us to the question: how is oppression to be

analysed? We are oppressed in different ways and for different reasons. There is racial oppression, class oppression, sex/gender oppression – amongst others. But how do we decide whether race, class or sex/gender should be prioritized? We need a theory that enables us to work out for ourselves which of these dynamics is more important than the others. The differences between the various forms of oppression, which have different objects, should be recognized. But what is the origin, the source of the oppression? Is it capitalism, 'Babylon' or patriarchy? And is there really one source from which all oppression is ultimately derived – could we stop all forms of oppression by just turning off some tap? Or could it be that we suffer from *overlapping* oppressions?

Black people are bitterly divided about the precise relationship of race and class and are continually asking themselves: should the struggle of black people be separate and autonomous? Should black people subsume the race struggle under the class struggle? Or should alliances, which allow some autonomy, be made with the working class? Before we look at the arguments of those blacks that stress class, let us consider the arguments of those that want to emphasize the autonomy of race, *the cultural separatist view*.

There are some political parties on the Left that are trying to raise the class consciousness of blacks. It is believed by some black people that these parties are being manipulative and wish to further the self-interests of whites. Having experienced working-class racism, many blacks stress the reactionary nature of the white working class.

What are the working-class views that black people 'hear'? 'We are becoming second-class citizens in our own country. We are being taken over. They are pushing us out.' And so the blacks are blamed for the problems in the neighbourhood. As Robert Miles has pointed out, this is because there is fierce competition in the inner cities over scarce resources, and black people provide an immediate 'explanation' for the decline of material production and living conditions.[17]

Miles has suggested that working-class racist beliefs are an attempt to understand and explain immediate daily experience. This is correct but shows the limitations of those theories that stress 'experience'. Now, marxism recognizes the value of experience but it goes further than this, it stresses the construction and use of abstract concepts (for example the forces and relations of production) to grasp the underlying structures and processes which cannot be grasped in terms of experience.

What I am arguing is this: black people know where they stand in relation to the political Right but it is with the supporters of the Left that they feel uneasy. After all, it was the Labour government that enforced legal restrictions against black immigrants. Moreover, the trade unions have not only taken no interest in the struggles of black people but have actually practised discrimination against them. Unfortunately, the British trade unions still focus on the 'core' working class, the middle-aged, skilled, white male worker. The unions do not now represent the working class in the way that they used to do and their strength has declined as so many of their former members are now unemployed. The leadership of the unions is still strongly resistant to making links with the new social movements.

It is easy for some sections of the Left to assert 'blacks and whites unite', but many black people are sceptical of such slogans and think that a class perspective is a white perspective. People's view of the world is rarely, if ever, ordered and consistent, and it is often the case that white workers have racist beliefs which coexist with expressions of class consciousness. I think it can be shown that the labour movement seriously underestimates the dimension of race and that the trade unions are permeated with racism.

Against this view, I suppose, it could be argued that we should not forget that there is a democratic tradition that comes from the labour movement and the unions. Many white, skilled men are learning about feminism and anti-racism. They often experience a tension between their male/national/racial chauvinism and the democratic principles promoted by the more radical elements in the movement and, gradually, they are becoming more aware.

Another argument black people use against the Left is this: a simple class analysis is reductionist because it excludes the fact that black people are not only exploited but are also oppressed. Many blacks are therefore sceptical of the Left and are organizing themselves in their own groups. They want to be autonomous because race has its own separate dynamic. But, as A. Sivanandan has argued, 'excessive autonomy leads us to inward struggles, awareness problems, consciousness raising and back again to the whole question of attitudes and prejudices.'[18] Of course, black people need to make use of the positive aspects of culture but too much autonomy leads to a form of cultural separatism.

Let us now turn to the arguments of those black groups that prioritize *the class view*. Many theorists contend that the roots of racism are to be found in imperialism. What other reason is there for people of West African origin being in the United States of America? Why are there so many people of Asian and Afro-Caribbean origin in Britain? Racial stereotypes and feelings of white superiority, all of which are strongly related to imperialism, are widespread in British culture. In fact, there is a relationship between imperialism, nationalism and racism. During the last seventy years, war has been the means of confirming and revalidating English nationalism, but with the advent of black immigration it has become possible to define Englishness vis-à-vis this internal 'enemy', this 'foreign body' in our own streets.[19] Thus the English, in identifying and setting apart the blacks, are asserting a nationalism through the means of racism.

Having already deprived the indigenous section of the working class of its basic needs, capital now deprives the working class further in order to exploit another section of it, the blacks. At the same time it prevents them both from coming to a common consciousness of class by intruding the consciousness of race. It prevents, in other words, the horizontal conflict of classes through the vertical integration of race and, in the process, exploits both race and class at once.[20]

What this means is that, whereas the working class sees itself exploited as a class and comes face to face with its exploiter, capital, the capitalist exploitation of blacks is veiled by racial oppression. As a result, they are caught up in a two-fold consciousness, as a class and as a race, each of which often contradicts the other. Adherents of this class perspective suggest that blacks should not isolate themselves;

as they form only 4 per cent of the population of Britain, black people should develop alliances with white workers and other groups. And so some black groups are seriously thinking of representation in the political party system; they argue that imperialism exploits blacks *and* whites and makes them one class. But there is a problem here: by entering conventional party politics, will blacks be incorporated into parliamentarism – a politics which has always been associated with bourgeois reformism? What would be the point of representation if blacks joined the ranks of the conservative or social-democratic parties? Blacks who want to prioritize class stress the important point that racial and other divisions are constantly being used by the capitalist state to divide the working class.

I regret the fact that some groups on the Left stress class to such an extent that other dynamics are ignored. On the issue of black people they do not recognize the importance of race. Again, on the issue of Northern Ireland, they stress class and completely neglect the question of religion. On the subject of feminism class is underlined but the sex/gender dynamic is ignored.

There is a bitter dissension about these matters and I think it is a pity that the different organizations do not see themselves as partners rather than competitors in the struggle for liberation. Infighting is depressing and unnecessary; I often think of the struggle in Spain, in the 1930s, where the anarchists and the communists, the atheists and the Jews fought against each other rather than their common enemy, and how this led to a tragic defeat.

I am sympathetic to the view that asserts that black people need to fight simultaneously as a people and as a class – as blacks and as workers – not by subsuming the race struggle under the class struggle but by deepening and broadening class struggle through its black and anti-colonial, anti-imperialist dimension. At the same time we must try and win the white working class for black struggles. The struggle against racism is the struggle for the class.

Political neutralization and the ideology of ethnicity

Let us now relate the discussion of race and class to the

ideological battle being fought out in the schools. In most of the advanced industrial states in the West which have exploited black labour the strategies used to contain black people form a pattern: at first, assimilation, then integration, and when that fails, 'cultural pluralism'.

Capital requires racism not for racism's sake but for the sake of capital. At a certain time it finds it more profitable to abandon the idea of superiority of race in order to promote the idea of 'cultural pluralism'. What are the methods used to politically neutralize blacks? Firstly, many black self-help groups are being bought off at the present time by the capitalist state in an attempt to stamp out the breeding grounds of resistance. This is an example of the strategy I mentioned earlier when I was discussing Gramsci's concept of hegemonic struggle: the political neutralization of opposition from a new social group by co-option of its political organizations.

Secondly, making a few blacks bourgeois so that they can support capitalism – the system that exploits the majority of them – is a well-known tactic to incorporate them. Let me give an example from some research on black women at British universities. The researcher, Sally Tomlinson, found that one of the factors that appear to have contributed to the 'success' of these students was the willingness to move house to better schools in a 'white area': 'In my sheltered middle-class area my parents were actually pleased I didn't know many blacks.' Tomlinson remarks that these students 'are likely to become a part of a small but growing black middle class in Britain, and since it was more highly educated blacks who led civil rights campaigns in the USA their influence may well be felt throughout the black community in Britain.'[21]

I am sceptical about this. I doubt whether the American civil rights movement has altered the *economic* position of blacks to any significant extent. All that has happened is that a few blacks have managed to gain access to economic resources and have ended up by supporting the status quo rather than challenging the whole basis of the capitalist system. These people have been allowed to move upwards within the existing system so that they would not threaten to transform it into a different system. They form a class of collaborators who justify the ways of the capitalist state to the blacks.

A third characteristic method of absorption and neutralization is by eliminating antagonisms and transforming them into simple differences. For example, the antagonisms white/black, bourgeoisie/proletariat are being transformed into a matter of cultural differences. This is 'cultural pluralism' and it is now the basis of multiracial education. Throughout this book I have argued that what is called 'multiracial education' is largely ideological. Even liberal writers are now admitting that it is a confidence trick.[22]

I don't want to be misunderstood. I am not saying that all reforms are sophisticated, managerial strategies – that would be a very limited view. I think 'reforms' such as MRE are an expression of struggle and that such 'discourses' can be appropriated by management, or reappropriated by socialist teachers for anti-racist teaching. A useful distinction is sometimes made between two forms of reaction: protest and resistance. Reactions of protest have the effect of supporting the continuation of the system. Reactions of resistance assume that the system as a whole is structurally at fault and that it neither possesses the ability nor the will to bring about the kind of changes demanded by resisting groups.[23]

I have noticed that in some recent books there is a romantic tendency to stress either 'black youth' as the vanguard, or the struggles of the 'community'. The former view has been vigorously stated by Farrukh Dhondy. While some teachers still believe that the schools are part of the welfare facilities that the British state offers its population, Dhondy believes that they have a policing function.[24] Teachers are workers who sell their labour power to produce graded and disciplined labour power. For him schools are political institutions in a crisis, and he rejoices in black youth's refusal of work discipline at school and their rejection of white culture. This is an expression of black resistance.

Other writers have located the centre of black struggles in the 'community'.[25] The impression often given is that a community exists out there as an undifferentiated mass, but this is not the case – there is no homogeneous black community. It should be remembered that within the black 'community' there are proletarian, petty-bourgeois and bourgeois sections. And just as race can be used to divide working-class unity, so class can be used to divide blacks. As Sivanandan has pointed out, a black bourgeoisie is now being fostered to act as a 'buffer' and to fragment black struggle. It seems that British state policy is changing from 'institutional' racism to what is called 'domestic neo-colonialism' – this refers to processes by which the state and its agents hand over control of black dissidents to the black bourgeoisie.

There is a constant struggle between competing conceptions of racial reality. In connection with reactions of protest, Mullard has coined the phrase phoney or colonial space and gives as examples the establishment of local community relations councils, the setting up of units and centres for multicultural education, and the provision of slots to discuss multicultural issues in the school curriculum. I agree with him that all these 'products' have been provided by powerful white groups as a response to *white* perceptions and definitions of what constitutes the problem in schools and society.

You may have noticed that I have avoided using the term 'ethnicity'. The reason is this: based on the ideology of cultural pluralism, ethnicity stresses not 'blacks' as a political cohesive group, but the characteristics of the constituent minorities, Afro-Caribbean, Asian, African, etc. Ethnicity focuses not on what exploited groups have in common but on their cultural differences.[26] In trying to remove the idea of group superiority while keeping the idea of group difference, ethnicity sidles into a culturalism which predicates separate but equal development, apartheid. Ethnicity, the new philosophy of separate development, masks the problem of racism and weakens the struggle against it. It changes a horizontal division of class into a vertical division of race and thereby undermines the class struggle. In short, the stress on ethnicity and cultural pluralism in multiracial education is a policy that attempts to undermine the underlying class aspect of black politics. It is the reaction of a system that is afraid that the black working-class struggles may begin to politicize the working class as a whole.

Now, liberals and social democrats stress the richness and diversity of black groups, the right of black groups settled here to full citizenship and equal treatment. But in supporting the ideology of cultural or ethnic pluralism, white reformists tend to subordinate racial to cultural factors and always minimize class considerations.

In the city ghettos the struggle is moving into a new phase with 'the blacks' representing a new social movement. They have a deep need to preserve their cultural identity rather than any wish to be represented in the traditional bourgeois parliamentary form. Unfortunately the Left is doing nothing to draw Afro-Caribbean and Asian people towards socialism (why doesn't the Labour Party create black sections?) Socialists have a vision of a new social order based on egalitarian principles of production and distribution and they want a revolutionary transformation of society. But the sad fact is that for most people socialism is still an abstract concept. And so we must ask: how do we transform socialist theory into political practice?

Chapter 9
Conclusions . . .

Re-vision: ideologies in multiracial education

In this penultimate chapter I present a summary of the key points of the book. The terse recapitulation of the main arguments provides the opportunity for reflection and enables me to suggest lines of thought about the policy recommendations that follow from what I have said.

Ideologies in multiracial education

The first chapter, a general introduction to multiracial education, discussed problems concerning pupils' behaviour, teachers' practices and expectations, and the school curriculum's effect on our view of other cultures. It was argued that racism was not just a matter of individual psychology, but that it was also structural, and that it is useful to distinguish three levels: personal racism, institutionalized racism and state racism.

This was followed by an historical outline of how state institutions and agencies have tried to impose their definitions on multiracial education. I described three models – the assimilationist, the integrationist, the cultural-pluralist – and the policies that flowed from them. There are remarkable similarities in the ideas of the sociologists, the psychologists and the government agencies. It is clear that educational theories and policies have been greatly influenced by two discourses: the racist assumptions of the sociology of 'race relations' and the psychological approach to multiracial education. The discourse of 'race relations' focuses on culture and ethnicity and avoids discussion of politics and economics. The psychological approach sees multiracial education as being about attitudes, dispositions, and respect for self and others.

It was stated that the educational failure of black children is *not* due to poor self-image or any other psychological factor. I agreed with Maureen Stone's view that multiracial education has become tied to a theory of cultural deprivation which finds it necessary to compensate black children for alleged deficiencies. Moreover, it is ethnocentric and aims at 'watering down' and 'cooling out' black inner-city children. Indeed, 'Black Studies' and the therapeutic teaching approach may have actually increased educational inequality. To put it concisely, schools are sponsoring black academic failure.[1]

I then made some criticisms of Stone's thesis. Though her central recommendation is the use of more formal methods of teaching West Indian children, she says nothing about the content of the curriculum, nor does she consider theories of knowledge. The main purpose of education seems to be to 'get on'; she writes of black people 'making the most of it to get out and move up'. This stress on social mobility leads her to a position of political reformism. There is nothing in her book about challenging the structures of capital. However, she perceptively writes, 'The school system has never reflected the culture of the majority of children in the country who are working class. Why then this concern to reflect the culture of small sections of that class – West Indian and other minority group children?' But she cannot answer her own question. This is because she does not see that multiracial education is a site of ongoing struggle between contending political forces. Because she is a social democrat, a reformist, she is unwilling to discuss the role of capital.[2] She also ignores capital's relationship to the state and how it exploits the social divisions of race, class and gender for its own advantage. In my view, the lack of a marxist analysis leads to serious limitations. For example, she separates education from politics; it is not surprising, then, that the themes of class struggle, political mobilization and the creation of a socialist hegemony are absent in her work.

Throughout the book I have been very critical of those who disseminate psychological and/or cultural-pluralist ideas in multiracial education, and of those who propagate a belief in 'equality of opportunity'. These powerful *ideologies* are being used to limit change. Perhaps I ought to remind you what I mean by ideology. Basically, an ideology involves the concealment of contradictions and, in doing so, it serves the interests of the ruling class.[3] Ideologies dehistoricize by treating existing social arrangements as eternal; things that are social are made to appear 'natural' and unproblematic. I believe that racism has been discussed for too long at the psychological level of personal feelings. The problem is not prejudice but domination. Racial practices must be considered within a context of *power* relationships.

Though many feminists make the point that sociology of education neglects gender, I have noticed that these white women themselves ignore the issue of race. A distinction was made between the work of marxist feminists and liberal/radical feminists in the sociology of education. I was very critical of the latter who call for 'equality of opportunity' rather than demand a fundamental change in society. These reformists explain oppression by patriarchy and pay no attention to the influence and effects of class and capital.

I attacked white feminism for its incipient racism and lack of relevance. Much of feminist theory, liberal and marxist, excludes black women. Black women at last are beginning to question the assumptions of white feminists. After all, the struggles and experiences of black women are different from those of white women because they have been structured by racism. Black women feel that the involvement of other British women in imperialism is repressed and the benefits that they – as whites – gained from the oppression of black people ignored.

Let us turn now to 'equality of opportunity'. The notion that all children, regardless of background, should have an equal chance to achieve in the education system contains a central contradiction. The inadequacy of this concept in the field of education and race relations arises from the fact that equality of opportunity cannot be achieved in a society that is fundamentally unequal, a society where people start off from positions of inequality vis-à-vis the structures of power and wealth. If society is differentiated on the basis of power, wealth and education, how can children coming into the educational system from various parts of that differentiated society ever, as it were, line up equally? I would argue that multiracial education based on 'equality of opportunity' directs attention away from those structures that create, maintain and reproduce inequality, and towards the individuals within those structures. This approach allows the structures of inequality to remain intact and yet gives the impression of doing something about this injustice.

In short, my argument is that all 'discourses' that ignore social structure and its reflection in the school system are false and dangerous. They are used as ideological diversion; they serve to deflect attention from the racist structures and practices of the British state and obscure the real issues of power, class and racial oppression.

There was then a discussion on schooling and I focused on the research by Mary Fuller which contradicts the general picture of West Indian disaffection from school and their low attainment. The black girls in the study showed (in contrast to the white working-class girls studied by McRobbie) that academic success and femininity can be reconciled. Fuller argues that black working-class people are subordinated in essentially the same way as their white counterparts, but to class subordination is added that based on race/colour. I criticized the area of double subordination; this simple, additive model lacks any notion of contradiction. I believe that black people face many contradictions which express themselves in different forms in different contexts. Moreover, black women are subject not to double, but to triple oppression: class, race and gender.

After arguing that racism and sexism are not similar (the 'objects' which have to be analysed are different as are the forms of analysis needed), I gave the reasons why I am hostile to some white feminist influences in multiracial education. The white feminist movement has a considerable bourgeois, reformist element which diverts and fragments political struggle within MRE. Secondly, most feminist theory is Eurocentric. Little attention has been given by white feminists to the lives of black women who have either been made invisible or marginalized and whose struggle for liberation has been ignored. It is vital that white women remove the racism that exists in their movements before they make their contribution to multiracial education.

Youth and unemployment

The disproportionate concentration of potentially militant young blacks and working-class youth among the unemployed presents a problem for the state. And so new forms of state intervention have come into being. I believe that the Manpower Services Commission is attempting to restructure the labour market – not just the unemployed – in line with Conservative economic policy. The MSC is actively redefining the relationship between 'education' and 'training'. I was very critical of the government's training initiatives and their ideological role. We are told that joblessness is due to a lack of motivation, experience or skill rather than the position young people occupy in the economy. Youth unemployment is defined as a problem of faulty supply. And so the education system is blamed; the real problem, the economic crisis, has been ideologically transformed into the crisis of employability. We are asked to look at the inadequacies of teachers and pupils rather than the irrationalities of capitalism.[4]

It was contended that the reproduction of the mental/ manual division is a central organizing principle of the school. The structural cause of working-class failure lies in the division of mental and manual labour. For most working-class people years of manual labour bring about not merely a lack of cultural skills and habits necessary for study but an ideology that legitimates failures among working-class people themselves who have come to accept the division between thinkers and doers as a natural one.

What can be done to counteract this divisive principle? Any fundamental change in education would seem to be dependent on the destruction of capitalist relations of production and the state which secures them.[5] But something urgently needs to be done now. There are demands by industry and the political Right that pupils be trained; they must be socialized into work-discipline and given useful skills. Now, socialist teachers are in a difficult position; they believe that there is an educational element in labour and that the appropriation of nature through work is good. Socialists realize that if they reject MSC schemes there are other teachers who will willingly operate them. The problem is that many teachers on the Left seem to have no policy that clearly differentiates them from the Right. What, in short, should be the view of socialist teachers about education and the economy, learning and labour?

In my view, socialist teachers cannot contract out of participating in these schemes. If they do, then a vacuum is created which the Right can fill with its own definitions. This has already happened in areas such as 'the family' and 'the nation'. Teachers must say clearly that the schemes are inadequately funded and resourced and that they are just not good enough; but, at the same time, they must use the contradictions *within* the schemes as a part of their political strategy. Though both the political Left and Right believe that learning must be integrated with labour, a clear distinction should be made. The Right defines these schemes in terms of a narrow training for manual labour. Socialist teachers, wanting to integrate theory and practice, learning and labour, must stress those aspects that will realize the full educational potentiality of all human beings.

I believe that there should be a continual challenge to the abstract nature of learning. Teachers should try and link learning with real life and relate their lessons to the experiences of pupils. Schooling must be made more relevant to the immediate needs of young people. It is clear that an education which linked learning with everyday experience, a high level of scientific, political, economic and general education for all and which fostered the integration of labour with learning would undermine the exclusion of the working class from the means of production. It is this exclusion that is the basis of capitalist relations of production.

105

Nation, race and class

At the moment knowledge is appropriated, controlled and mystified by capital, but in a socialist society there would be a dialetical unity between mental and manual labour, and the mass of the population, each and all, would participate in the running and organization of production *and* society. This was the vision that was held by Antonio Gramsci.

He argued that ideology is for binding people together to motivate them politically, and that class domination is exercised as much through popular consensus as through force. Thus, political, intellectual and moral leadership leads to hegemony.

I then explained the ideas of Ernesto Laclau and Chantal Mouffe who, greatly influenced by Gramsci, also see politics as the struggle to achieve hegemony. They argue that social classes do not have pure, paradigmatic ideologies. Ideological elements in isolation have no necessary class connotation. In other words, class elements of an ideology cannot be predicted – it depends on how particular elements are put together. They insist that the class character of an ideology is given not by its content but by its *form*. Politics, in part, consists of the struggle over the relationship between the elements. Ideological struggle, then, consists of a process of disarticulation of given ideological elements in a struggle between two hegemonic principles to appropriate these elements. Laclau and Mouffe assert that every class struggles at the ideological level simultaneously as class and as 'the people'. That is to say, class objectives are presented as the consummation of popular objectives.

We then considered nationalism. Many marxists believe that nationalism is an element of bourgeois ideology and is not susceptible to transformation in a socialist direction. Laclau and Mouffe, however, argue that nationalism, considered by itself, has no class connotation – the latter only derives from its specific articulation with other ideological elements. One of our main tasks, therefore, must be the disarticulation of its democratic elements and their rearticulation to working-class ideology.

I expressed some reservations about the work of Laclau and Mouffe because they have an idealist tendency to collapse all practices into one discursive practice. They ignore the extra-discursive. Their work neglects economic contradictions and constraints, material inducements and the power of the repressive state apparatus. Though in some ways they are revisionists, I find their insights valuable when used to analyse ideological struggles concerning nation, race and class.

Drawing on the work of Laclau and Mouffe it is possible to understand why there is a continual stress in parliament, the media and elsewhere on 'the British nation' – an ideological construct that deliberately excludes blacks. The Left, because it has always tended to stress internationalism, has never been able to deal with the discourse of nationalism adequately. My argument is simply this: there is an urgent need to disarticulate some of the elements of this right-wing nationalist discourse and rearticulate them in a popular, socialist ideology that integrates the discourses of class, race *and* nation. There must be a recognition that a Left populist struggle needs Afro-Caribbean and Asian organizations and other groups and movements.

I then mentioned some of the ways in which blacks are being politically neutralized. State-sponsored organizations are being used to defuse black resistance. An attempt is being made to divert black people into supporting community relations measures and 'race relations' legislation. Many of the organizations associated with these projects seem to assume that the problems are not racial but community ones. They do not see their job in terms of righting wrong but of preventing 'trouble'. Racism, they say, is not a white problem but a human one. In this process these organizations attempt to co-opt the small professional layer amongst the black population in order to channel the struggles of black people into reformism. And so a black bourgeoisie, a class of collaborators is being formed.

Meanwhile, in the schools, children are being socialized through multicultural education into accepting 'cultural pluralism'. This approach is fashionable at the moment and I am very critical of it. I have explained how the term 'multicultural' gives the impression that many groups with different but equally strong interests can fairly compete in a contest where the state is 'neutral', above the struggle. Now,

107

the pluralist idea is similar; it emphasizes the consensual and assumes that all groups within society possess equal amounts of power. The concept of *ethnicity* is playing an increasingly important role in multiracial education. My contention is that the ethnic identity of black groups is being fostered (not only in the schools but in the media) because it focuses not on what exploited groups have in common but on their differences. The emphasis on ethnicity hides the fact that there is a force which exercises power, which fragments, exploits and oppresses other groups such as blacks, women and workers.

Anti-racist teaching

I believe that multiracial education as *practised* in most British schools is mere tokenism. Though many schools have anti-racist policy documents and guidelines these remain formal and are not put into operation. One constraint on teachers is that they are expected to present a 'balanced view'. Robert Jeffcoate's views can be given as an example of what I mean.[6] He has a dislike of what he sees as political indoctrination and so he opposes even affective goals like interracial respect. He believes that children should feel able to express their racism in classroom discussion and also that teachers should avoid adopting a censorious attitude in these cases: 'Young white racists have as much right as anyone else to expect to find attentive adult ears at school . . . [they] for the most part, need support and sympathy, not gagging.' Is this a 'balanced' view of race?

Urban schools have always been sites of political and ideological struggle.[7] Every day a battle for consciousness is going on between those who want to preserve the status quo and those who want to change society. But we know that schools were not set up to develop critical consciousness. One consequence is that 'race' as a political issue is never discussed. As teachers have not been prepared to teach politics, many of them slip back into a notion of 'professional' neutrality. The presence of the police, the church and the army (and their ideologies) in schools is taken for granted, accepted as normal – but anti-racist work is regarded as dangerous. I want to argue that a clear distinction should be made between multiracial education and anti-racist teaching; the former stresses cultural features that are 'safe', the latter is contentious because it is *political*.

At the present time teachers are working under enormous pressures. Schools are being closed or amalgamated, resources are being cut, teacher morale is low. To be asked to concentrate on anti-racist teaching at such a time is often perceived as yet another burden. And yet those teachers who are doing good work are often unfairly criticized. I know some who have been accused of increasing racial tension by drawing attention to racial discrimination. Anti-racist teaching is seen as legitimate if it is done, for example, in 'social studies'. If such teaching can be hived off to a place where it is a safe, known category, unable to infect other areas, then it is 'all right'.

I believe that to fully understand the whole, contradictory situation – the encouragement of a serious multiracial policy by a few educational authorities within a capitalist state that is deeply racist – we must place this discussion in the context of the Thatcherite offensive against state education.

The attack on state education

One of the most important developments during the last ten years has been the attack on state education. Conservatives have identified 'popular' educational issues such as parental rights, the notion of choice, success defined as exam performance, the quality of teaching and teacher training, and made them largely their own – irrespective of the effects of their own policies. They have championed selection and the private sector rather than the comprehensive schools where most children get their schooling.[8] Most commentators are agreed that the aim of the Conservatives is to roll back and eventually remove the state as the main provider of social and educational services. To put it concisely, the Right has been allowed to define the areas of educational concern and set the terms of the debate. Its campaign about education has been successful because it has related in important ways to elements of popular experience.

Since the mid-1970s a growing number of people have realized that comprehensive schooling has failed to correct existing patterns of educational inequality. Many parents have felt excluded from any participation in the activities of the schools. There has been no questioning or assessment of the traditional school curriculum; in fact, most black and working-class pupils feel debarred from the cultural values it embodies. Indeed, for an increasing number of young working-class people schooling is a deeply alienating experience – as it was for their parents.

Many of the tendencies, such as centralization of control, which I have described in this book will undoubtedly continue during the next few years, especially if a right-wing government is in power. Conservatives, on the whole, believe that educational systems are formed because of the conflict between status groups (not social classes). For them there is no opposition between capital and civil society. Educational change is the result of a change in market forces or of natural evolution.

There are several overlapping strands in Conservative educational policy. One of them, Thatcherism, which has been characterized as 'authoritarian populism', wishes to restore inequality by separating the 'deserving' from the 'undeserving'. Thatcherism is as dismissive of the poor as it is of the Tory aristocracy. In education it supports the move towards privatization, a policy which removes responsibility from the state and thus helps its legitimation. There is a shift away from social welfare; it is said 'people should stand on their own feet and not require a welfare state to support them'. Many of the things that were formerly done by the state have now to be done in the family. And as the autonomy of the teacher decreases, schools are becoming more open to the pressures from industry and middle-class parents.

The thrust towards a more 'efficient' education system will mean increasing 'rationalization' and government control ('accountability'). Whilst outside the state system there will be a stress on private education, within the state system there will be moves towards a common-core curriculum, a return to 'basics'. The Manpower Services Commission will almost certainly gain more influence as unemployment increases. Within schools training, as opposed to education, will become more overt and pervasive. And, of course, coinciding with these developments, there will be an emphasis on moral regeneration – after all, it costs nothing.

What about race? I have argued that all liberal models of education assume various degrees of cultural change on the part of black groups in school and society without any corresponding change on the part of white groups. The 'multicultural' educational models are in fact power models constructed by dominant white groups for the protection of their power. Even the most well-intentioned multicultural initiatives have functioned as a means of diffusing difficult inner-city school situations and as an attempt to pacify black communities. As interpreted and practised by many teachers, multicultural education has become an instrument of control and stability rather than of change. It has fostered the cultural subordination and the political neutralization of blacks.

I believe that the current trend in multiracial education, the stress on *ethnicity* and the cultural values of different minority groups, will continue. This is yet another liberal approach which concentrates on life-styles and persistently ignores anything that may increase life chances. The ethnic identity of black groups is fostered whilst, at the same time, they are prevented by the dominant class from gaining positions of power in the major institutions of the state.

Chapter 10

. . . and beginnings

Introduction

Education is being 'restructured' and schools are being increasingly brought under control – but by whom? Some writers, like Salter and Tapper, have suggested that there is more and more control of education by the Department of Education and Science.[1] The DES is increasingly involved in cost-benefit analysis and sophisticated management systems which tend to justify the need for greater control. There is greater DES intervention in the curriculum and there is also considerable inspectorate activity in monitoring education 'standards'. Whilst what the authors say is true, I think they exaggerate the power of the DES and neglect the role and strength of the MSC.

It seems that while the broad thrust of government policy is clear, different government departments and ministers interpret that policy and its implications for education in rather different ways. I agree with Roger Dale's suggestion that to really know how political decisions affecting education are taken we need a theory of the state and an understanding of the operation of the state apparatus as a whole.[2] We should bear in mind the historical specificity of the education state apparatus and the relationships between education, policymaking and what goes on in schools.

And so, what is to be done? I think that it is important that we work out for ourselves what we consider to be the role of the teacher and the function of schooling in capitalist

112

society. We must theorize and adopt a coherent position, otherwise pressures from other groups and sources will impose themselves on us. Having a developed theoretical position is equivalent to having a set of principles which prevent one drifting from one pragmatic position to another.

School-community relations

This chapter, which contains practical suggestions for overcoming racism, will focus on school-community relations, the training of teachers, and proposals for the construction of a new curriculum. We need a plan of action both at the macro and the micro level. We need to make changes in the structures and the practices of the state and its institutions such as the Department of Education and Science and the Manpower Service Commission, local education authorities and the schools.

At the present time local education authorities have not got a well-developed theory or a coherent policy concerning race, class and gender.[3] This is partly because the political parties are not in touch with the grassroots. Some important changes are beginning to take place in the schools but the political parties of the Left have not yet realized this.

Priority must be given to establishing close links between the school and the community, between the teachers, pupils, the non-teaching staff and the community outside, the parents, the voluntary groups and the official organizations. Schools should be opened up to the outside community who should have access to its facilities. As teachers we must have a practical willingness to work with those who, like black parents, have many criticisms of the system and its teachers. I think we must actively encourage black parents and submit the structures of the education system and our practices to criticism by them.

Parents should not only know about the content of the curriculum but should also contribute to it. I believe that schools should utilize the knowledge and expertise of the parents to the full. In a truly multiracial society mutual understanding between the community and the school is vital. Any new strategy must involve those whom it will affect.

Sometimes I hear the suggestion that black communities should set up their own separate schools where they can learn the knowledge and skills required to gain access to positions of power and control. Setting up separate ethnic schools may be one way of bypassing official obstruction. But it should be remembered that though 'ethnic' diversity is seen as delightfully interesting and enriching as long as it is not a threat, once these schools show black groups how to demand and obtain resources, then it might well be said that they are going too far and are a threat to 'the core values of the nation'. But I have a more immediate concern and it is this: if blacks were institutionally separate, would they *all* gain educationally? Many of the schools might well be only for the rich, and so I do not support the idea of separate institutions but believe that it is vital for black groups to demand radical improvements in the state system.

Anti-racist teacher training

In order to improve school-community relations I want to make four proposals that could be implemented immediately.

(1) As educational institutions should reflect the multi-racial society we live in, *more black people should be encouraged to enter the teaching service.* There should, firstly, be more 'access' courses for blacks so that they can qualify for entry into teacher training. Secondly, there should be positive discrimination on behalf of black teachers. This should be more than tokenism. Too often black teachers are ghettoized; they meet with prejudice from their white colleagues, headteachers block their promotion chances, and they are kept unfairly on the lower rungs of the pay ladder.

We must do something about the processes which result in black people teaching black youngsters in Hackney and white people teaching white youngsters in Hampstead. Perhaps a certain number of teaching posts could be reserved for black teachers in each local authority. No doubt it will be said against the above proposal that there are many qualified teachers who are unemployed and competition is already intense because of staff redundancies, falling rolls and school amalgamations.

(2) *No white person who is racist should be allowed to enter the teaching profession.* I realize the difficulty of putting this proposal into practice. Some people, for example, might argue that attitude tests are difficult to devise because of differing definitions of racism. Moreover, there are some aspects of racism that are not manifest at an overt level during screening procedures. But, on the other hand, what would be the point of a multicultural curriculum if it was taught by persons who were racially prejudiced?

Some people assert that there is racial discrimination amongst blacks themselves, that black people prefer amongst their own people those with lighter pigmentation. (See, for example, the advertisements for arranged marriages in Indian newspapers.) The paradigm of beauty that some black people admire is the Greco-Roman. Cultural imposition takes many forms and one wonders whether such an attitude could have come about through the internalization by the Slave of the values of the Master?[4]

This is a sensitive area because this view is often taken to extremes by whites who believe that blacks are ugly and actually assume that blacks think so, too. Perhaps, at one time, there were some blacks who felt physically inferior because of the power of the dominant definition. The 'black is beautiful' movement can be seen as a reaction against any self-denigration. If there is discrimination amongst blacks themselves regarding skin colouration, it must be dealt with.[5] I believe that the task of the teacher is to debunk racist interpretations by offering alternatives and to work to alter the reality of the situation itself.

(3) *All teacher training should include compulsory courses on multiracial education.* All students should be prepared for teaching in multiethnic classrooms and they should have experience in making anti-racist material. The training of teachers should include some interdisciplinary work so that they do not feel threatened when they have to integrate their discipline with other subjects. Many younger children in secondary schools are taught in an interdisciplinary way but, unfortunately, by the fifth year there is a reversion to a

115

traditional approach as the teaching becomes more examination-orientated.

There should be regular in-service courses whose purpose should be to make all those who work in schools examine the nature of institutional discrimination itself, that is to say, the form of discrimination established in the procedures and underlying assumptions on which the schools themselves are organized. These courses should be organized – and monitored – by black teachers. Of course, some people may doubt the effectiveness of such training. Even when everything has been explained, residues of racism may still exist. I come across many teachers who don't want to confront white racism and therefore focus on quaint aspects of other cultures. Multiculturalism, then, is not enough; education for a multicultural society must be anti-racist.

(4) *Those teachers that behave in a racist way should be disciplined and their acts considered legal offences.* Many teachers may say that such a measure is not required, that any misdemeanours can be corrected within the profession. Anyway, how is one to decide on the seriousness of the offence and how does one 'prove' racial prejudice and discrimination? I believe that teachers should be accountable to the community and that criteria can be instituted which would give support to the work of anti-racist teachers.

The above policies should be carried out not only at school but at community, local authority and national level. Right-wing groups will vehemently reject these ideas; but then they always stress the values of the dominant group and pathologize the views of subordinate groups. I want to insist on the importance of these concrete proposals because I can see when I am supervising my students on teaching practice that multiracial education, after all these years, is still having no impact in schools.

The above suggestions may seem radical, but they are, in fact, the same recommendations that Lord Scarman wanted to be implemented by the police force in Britain.[6]

Towards a new curriculum

I have suggested in this book that the school curriculum,

based as it is on white cultural values, is something black youth cannot identify with. It is, indeed, one of the means by which racism is perpetuated. This was demonstrated by looking at a representative example of institutionalized racism, the teaching of geography, and its treatment of the 'Third World'.

In my view, socialist teachers should challenge the assumptions and contents of traditional curricula. They should begin questioning traditional dichotomies such as the division between academic study and manual training; between the hard, 'masculine' subjects like mathematics and the sciences, and the soft, 'feminine' arts subjects. They should question why a largely Anglocentric curriculum is still being offered in a society with a rich diversity of cultures. I maintain that students should be taught the new structuralist and semiological techniques of reading texts so that they can analyse the hidden curriculum of the school.

It is vital that teachers work collectively with colleagues to change the content of the curriculum. This would mean that they would have to make their own teaching materials rather than use what has been sold to them. Of course, this is already happening – I know some teachers who are working terribly hard developing new curricula to overcome race, sex and class discrimination. They are trying to show their colleagues the importance of developing new initiatives, but they are given little time and few resources to do this work.

As I believe that there must be a concerted policy of curriculum innovation I would like to provide a brief sketch of the main features of a new curriculum. I contend that all young people should learn philosophy and economics. Only a narrow Anglo-Saxon version of philosophy is taught in Britain at the moment. This will have to change. I envisage the teaching in schools of historical and dialectical materialism and of not only European but also Asian and African philosophies.[7] The study of dialectics would be an important element in such courses.[8] One implication of these innovations would be that every school subject would have to be rethought and the syllabus taught from a materialist point of view.

Students should be made aware that the outward appearance and the essence of things do not directly coincide – our ideas about reality can be mistaken and false. Progressivism honours the experience of the learners, of the excluded classes. But to be confined to one's own 'experience is to know the world one-dimensionally. It would be pointed out that traditional thought is based on dualistic distinctions (such as mental and manual labour, pure and applied science, agency and structure) and that this must be superseded. The new curriculum would stress the teaching of techniques that penetrate beyond appearances. Students have to be inspired with the notion that hard work is required to gain knowledge. Hard work is entailed in learning how to work on experience and 'theorize', how to use dialectics and construct new concepts.

At the present time there is a hierarchical division between mental and manual labour. In schools this split is usually thought of in terms of the 'academic' and the 'vocational'. I have argued against vocationalism because it perpetuates the elitist division between mental and manual labour, between active producers and passive consumers. This view, with its stress on relevance, is often called instrumentalism. But why should the majority of the population be restricted to merely manual training?

Some socialists who are opposed to instrumentalism go to the other extreme and adopt the slogan 'education for leisure'. This view is inadequate because it also relegates students to being alienated consumers. It is assumed that education is some sort of diversion or entertainment. It is my contention that both vocationalism and education for leisure are contemporary variants of anti-intellectualism. But an academic curriculum based on specialization in a narrow range of subjects will not do either. Such a curriculum provides a way of policing which social groups are allowed access to prestigious forms of knowledge and which have 'training' imposed upon them.

In the new curriculum an attempt would be made to integrate the mental and the manual; there would be a stress on the unity of theory and practice. The basis of such a curriculum would be the idea that work is a necessary feature of human life. In work we translate our subjective purposes and intentions into reality, we realize them and embody them in things.[9] When our efforts are united with the forces of production in a socialist society we will produce a better quality of life for everyone.

Another element in the new curriculum should be a basic course in economics. What is needed is an explanation of how neo-colonialism maintains and reproduces the conditions of poverty, unemployment and underdevelopment.[10] The underlying material, political and economic causes of racism must be fully understood by the teacher and explained to students.

I feel strongly that there are three phenomena that have been 'repressed' in the school curriculum: war, military violence and the role of the nation state. Why are so many teachers unconcerned about them? Why this silence? The nation state, which began in Europe, has become a global system. Industrial power and military power have combined in the nation state and now, tragically, the poorer countries of the 'developing' world are buying armaments from the more 'advanced' industrial nations. With the possession of nuclear weapons we have entered a new era. The means of waging wars are continually increasing and there are no mechanisms for controlling the proliferation of nuclear weapons. And so we are the first generation in history that may be destroyed in its entirety as a consequence of direct violence. Should not young people know all this?

Most people think of violence as if it always referred to something direct and personal, for example, terrorism, riots or war. But students should know that besides direct violence there are forms of *indirect* violence in our society which are structural. Structural violence includes discrimination against blacks (for example, apartheid), poverty, injustice. The absence of direct violence leads to what can be called a negative concept of peace, but the absence of indirect, structural violence leads to a 'positive' concept of peace.

To recapitulate, courses must be provided on the international world economy which is one of the main sources of racism today. We cannot hope to understand racism without a global perspective. This includes the study of a wide range of issues such as the role of multinational corporations, world unemployment, law and order, the military-industrial complex, the trade in arms and the arms race, and the nature of violence in the modern world.

Dismantling racism

More and more teachers are beginning to see that there are deep contradictions between what is happening on the ideological level in curriculum policy – a move towards a greater appreciation of the diverse cultures of black people – and the increasingly repressive policies of the state and its apparatuses in race relations. Not only has the state moved to more direct, overt and authoritarian forms of social control, but it has used race to secure hegemonic control in a period of crisis. It is evident that there is now a close link between the schools, the social services and the *police* with the aim of disciplining black youth.

During the last few years we have witnessed an increasing centralization and concentration of the police force. The changes in the character of the police have been introduced with little or no public debate in parliament or elsewhere. There are the signs of a gradual drift to a more authoritarian form of state.[11]

Following Gramsci, I would argue that state power ultimately rests upon force, but it is rarely used openly; instead, consent is relied upon. The two wings of state power, coercion and consent, are interdependent and the coercive interventions are successful because they are validated by the consent of the majority. A hegemonic crisis precipitates a shift towards coercion and, since this in itself would be likely to undermine popular consent, a new consent must be engineered which legitimates the use of the repressive state apparatus.

This raises many questions. For example, are the police a democratic force or are they the instrument of class or state oppression? I would argue that the lack of democratic control indicates that the police are a class force, serving not the people as a whole but the interests of the bourgeoisie. But this does not mean that the police are merely the instrument of the dominant class or that the character of the police is fixed by their class function. Rather the nature of the police depends on the relations *between* the classes, on the outcome of class struggles and on the influence which the working class and its allies manage to wield. Thus those who argue that the police are simply a democratic force ignore the actual insulation of the police from democratic control. Those who argue that the police are simply a class instrument ignore the different forms of police that emerge out of class struggle.[12] Now, what I have said about the police force applies equally to the role and function of *the teaching force:* its nature depends on the relations between the classes and is the outcome of class struggles.

The ruling capitalist class which controls the means of production, the means of persuasion and the means of coercion ruthlessly attempts to reduce democracy. It is continually making efforts to 'curb the trade unions', to increase the power of the repressive state apparatuses and to limit its accountability to the public. The working class, however, is always trying to increase popular democracy. As a part of the labour movement progressive teachers should endeavour to increase democratic processes in schools and society.

I know that teachers feel isolated in their school activities. And because teachers work with children in schools, all day, every day, there is a tendency for many of them to become *over-school-centred*. Now, I believe that schools do make a difference, schools can contribute to social change – *but they can only go so far.* This point is often forgotten by young teachers.

I therefore want to suggest that our analysis of education should be related to broader political struggles. One way of overcoming the isolation is by forming groups and learning to work collectively. A beginning could be made by making closer contact with the community and by organizing the curriculum according to the material interests of minority groups. This is one way in which anti-racist teaching could be linked to a discussion with pupils and parents about issues such as alienation, environmental damage, violence, poverty and injustice.

As schools can contribute to social change only to a limited extent, teachers should intensify the struggle on a

121

larger number of sites. They should be developers of 'critical consciousness' amongst their communities. They must link up with other teachers, not only in their staff-rooms and teacher centres, but in unions and political parties. I know it is hard for the classroom teacher to replace the habits of individualism by collective discussion and political action. But it must be done if anti-racist practices are to be established in this country. In short, *teachers must develop a political base outside the profession* so that their work is not easily marginalized. We must remember that the destruction of the existing division of labour and the abolition of race, sex and class inequalities is a *political,* not an educational goal.

Teachers must therefore continue their criticisms of the internal contradictions of capitalism, as this is a precondition for understanding schooling. We have to convince the black community that to subordinate the class struggle to the race struggle leads to barren cultural separatism, while at the same time convincing the Left that it is wrong to subordinate the race struggle to the class struggle. We have to offer a vision of schools, society and socialism that will fire the imagination not only of parents, teachers and students but of everyone.

How do *you* think we should combine theoretical imagination and political strategy?

That's all for now. Take care.

Love
Madan

Notes and references

Chapter 1 Multiracial education in the school

1 See, for example, Aaron V. Cicourel, *Method and Measurement in Sociology*, New York, Free Press, 1964, p. 185.
2 Salman Rushdie, 'The new empire within Britain', *New Society*, December 1982, p. 417.
3 Sigmund Freud, *Jokes and their Relation to the Unconscious*, Standard Edition, vol. 8, London, Hogarth Press, 1953–66. My understanding of jokes has been greatly extended by Trevor Griffiths's play *The Comedians*.
4 Dick Hebdige, *Subculture: The Meaning of Style*, London, Methuen, 1979.
5 Stuart Hall et al., *Policing the Crisis: Mugging, the State and Law and Order*, London, Macmillan, 1978.
6 C. Jones and K. Kimberley, 'Educational responses to racism', in John Tierney (ed.), *Race, Migration and Schooling*, London, Holt, Rinehart & Winston, 1982, p. 143.
7 The classic study of how teachers' beliefs about pupils may act as self-fulfilling prophecies is R. Rosenthal and L. Jacobson, *Pygmalion in the Classroom*, New York, Holt, Rinehart & Winston, 1968.
8 Note that the word 'denigrate', of Latin origin, has racist connotations, like many words we use without thinking of their origin.
9 Dawn Gill, *Assessment in a Multicultural Society, Schools Council Report: Geography*, London, Commission for Racial Equality, 1982. This report, rejected by the Schools Council, is obtainable from the Education Officer, Commission for Racial Equality (CRE), 10–12 Allington Street, London SW1E 5EH, tel. 01-828-7022.
10 Many of the images from the 'Third World' reinforce the negative stereotypes already existing in the British context. See Patricia Holland, ' "Save the Children" . . . or how the newspapers present pictures of children from the Third World', *Multiracial Education*, vol. 9, no. 2, 1981. This issue deals with race and the media.

11 Robert Jeffcoate, *Positive Image: Towards a Multiracial Curriculum,* London, Writers' and Readers' Publishing Co-operative / Chameleon Books, 1979.

Chapter 2   Racism and education

1 See Terence Hawkes, *Structuralism and Semiotics,* London, Methuen, 1977, p. 133.
2 This section draws on Chris Mullard, 'Multiracial education in Britain: from assimilation to cultural pluralism', in John Tierney (ed.), *Race, Migration and Schooling,* London, Holt, Rinehart & Winston, 1982.
3 Roy Jenkins, *Address Given by the Home Secretary to a Meeting of Voluntary Liaison Committees,* London, National Council for Commonwealth Immigrants (NCCI), 1966.
4 This has been called the 'moral education approach'. For a useful analysis of technicist, moral and socio-political policy see Jenny Williams, 'perspectives on the multi-cultural curriculum', *Social Science Teacher,* vol. 8, no. 4, 1979.
5 A useful introduction to state theory is Bob Jessop, *The Capitalist State,* Oxford, Martin Robertson, 1982.
6 S.M. Elkins, *Slavery. A Problem in American Institutional and Intellectual Life,* Chicago, University of Chicago Press, 1959.
7 Errol Lawrence, 'Sociology and black "pathology" ', in Centre for Contemporary Cultural Studies, *The Empire Strikes Back: Race and Racism in 70s Britain,* London, Hutchinson, 1982, p. 134.
8 Alan James and Robert Jeffcoate, *The School in the Multiracial Society,* London, Harper & Row, 1981, p. 12.
9 Ibid., p. 20.
10 Ibid., p. 189.
11 Ibid., p. 205.
12 Ibid., p. 7.
13 Ibid., p. 9.
14 Ibid., p. 8.
15 Ibid., p. 12.
16 Louis Althusser, 'Ideology and ideological state apparatuses', in Louis Althusser, *Lenin and Philosophy and other Essays,* London, New Left Books, 1971. This essay also appears in B.R. Cosin (ed.), *Education: Structure and Society,* Harmondsworth, London, Penguin, 1972.
17 Ibid., p. 28.

Chapter 3   Children and racial attitudes

1 David Milner, *Children and Race,* Harmondsworth, Penguin, 1975, and *Children and Race: Ten Years On,* London, Ward Lock Educational, 1983.
2 Ibid., p. 121.

3 Ibid., p. 137.
4 Ibid., p. 144.
5 Ibid., p. 140.
6 Ibid., p. 148.
7 For a critique of Milner and the doll studies see Maureen Stone, *The Education of the Black Child in Britain: The Myth of Multiracial Education,* London, Fontana, 1981, pp. 53–6.
8 The dialectical nature of human relationships is expressed, for example, in Hegel's story of the Master and the Slave. He remarks that in the life and death fight one of the adversaries gives in to the other and submits to him without being recognized by him. The Master makes the Slave work to satisfy his own desires; but to satisfy these desires of the Master, the Slave has to repress his own instincts, to negate or 'overcome' himself as a given. The Slave transcends himself by working, or to put it in a better way, he educates himself. In his work he transforms things and transforms himself at the same time. In becoming master of Nature by work, the Slave frees himself from Nature, from his own nature, and from the Master. It is because work is an auto-creative act that it can raise him from slavery to freedom. The difference between Master and Slave exists only at the beginning and can be overcome in the course of time. Man is not born slave or free but creates himself as one or the other through action. The thesis of Mastery and the antithesis of Slavery are thus dialectically 'overcome'. The future and history belong not to the warlike Master but to the working Slave.
I find it helpful to think of 'the fight among adversaries' as referring to the long struggle between whites and blacks. In the era of imperialism the blacks submitted to whites and were forced to work. The blacks/the oppressed transcend themselves by working – they educate themselves. Through work and struggle the oppressed blacks free themselves. Mastery and Slavery, then, are not given, they are not innate characteristics. We create ourselves. All of history is nothing but the progressive negation of Slavery by the oppressed. Finally, both Mastery and Slavery are dialectically overcome by revolution.
In this paragraph I have drawn on Alexandre Kojève, *Introduction to the Reading of Hegel,* assembled by Raymond Queneau, New York, Basic Books, 1969. It is a commentary on Hegel's *Phenomenology of Spirit.*
9 Milner, op. cit., p. 149.
10 Ibid., p. 157.
11 Ibid., p. 163.
12 Ibid., p. 192.
13 Ibid., p. 34.
14 Ibid., p. 2.
15 I am thinking of a speech like the following:

> 'If we went on as we are, then by the end of the century there would be 4 million people of the New Commonwealth or Pakistan here. Now, that is an awful lot and I think it means that people are really rather afraid that this country might be swamped by people with a

different culture. And, you know, the British character has done so much for democracy, for law, and done so much throughout the world that, if there is a fear that it might be swamped, people are going to react and be rather hostile to those coming in.'

Margaret Thatcher, October 12, 1979

Chapter 4 The education of the black child

1 Maureen Stone, *The Education of the Black Child in Britain*, London, Fontana, 1981. The title is somewhat misleading as the book is a study only of the West Indian child.
2 See, for example, David Milner, *Children and Race*, London, Penguin, 1975.
3 Stone, op. cit., pp. 71–86.
4 Bernard Coard, *How the West Indian Child is Made Educationally Subnormal in the British School System*, London, New Beacon Books, 1971.
5 Antonio Gramsci, *The Prison Notebooks*, London, Lawrence & Wishart, 1971.
6 Stone, op. cit., p. 100.
7 Paulo Freire, *Pedagogy of the Oppressed*, Harmondsworth, Penguin, 1972. He argues that traditional schooling is premised on what he calls the banking method – the idea that a student is an *object* into which knowledge is placed, not a *subject* in the learning process.
8 Stone, op cit., p. 88.
9 Ibid., p. 89.
10 Ibid., p. 66.
11 Ibid., p. 36.
12 Bob Jessop, *The Capitalist State,* London, Martin Robertson, 1982.
13 See, for example, Anne Showstack Sassoon (ed.), *Approaches to Gramsci,* London, Writers' and Readers' Publishing Co-operative, 1982.

Chapter 5 Knowledge, the curriculum and racism

1 P.H. Hirst, *Knowledge and the Curriculum*, London, Routledge & Kegan Paul, 1974. P.H. Hirst and R.S. Peters, *The Logic of Education*, London, Routledge & Kegan Paul, 1970.
2 For a critique of the philosophy of education of Peters and Hirst see Kevin Harris, *Education and Knowledge*, London, Routledge & Kegan Paul, 1979.
3 Michael F.D. Young (ed.), *Knowledge and Control*, London, Collier Macmillan, 1971.
4 See, for example, J. Beck, C. Jenks, N. Keddie and M.F.D. Young (eds), *Worlds Apart: Readings for a Sociology of Education*, London, Collier Macmillan, 1976.

5 S. Bowles and H. Gintis, *Schooling in Capitalist America,* London, Routledge & Kegan Paul, 1976.
6 In a recent article Bowles and Gintis admit that one of the weaker aspects of their book was their inadequate treatment of the systemic contradictions of advanced capitalism. Rejecting their earlier espousal of a simplistic base/superstructure model, they now formulate a concept of society as 'an ensemble of structurally articulated sites of social practice' (a view that reminds me of Althusser's concept of 'relative autonomy'). They assert that the three major sites are capitalist production, the state and the family system. Though the family is described as the site of patriarchy they fail to recognize that capitalist production is also the site of dominance of men over women. In the article the state is unquestioningly accepted as being democratic: in contrast to the rights vested in property at the site of production, 'political practices in the liberal democratic state are characterized by rights vested in persons, according to which all individuals as citizens participate equally in the determination of state decisions.' Having said that political equality has already been achieved for all, Gintis and Bowles argue that the dynamic of social struggle occurs 'wholly within the liberal discourse of natural rights'. Their view of liberal discourse draws on Wittgenstein's apolitical notion of rules and 'language games' and is based on a non-marxist view of the state as being neutral and democratic. But as Poulantzas pointed out, concepts such as 'equality' and 'rights' are catchwords under which bourgeois class exploitation entered and ruled in history. Gintis and Bowles do not realize that liberal discourse actually conceals class exploitation in a specific manner to the extent that all trace of class domination is systematically absent from its language. See Herbert Gintis and Samuel Bowles, 'Contradiction and reproduction in educational theory', in Roger Dale et al., *Education and the State, Volume 1: Schooling and National Interest,* Lewis, Falmer Press, 1981.
7 Paul Willis, *Learning to Labour,* Farnborough, Saxon House, 1977. See pp. 47–9 for a section on the racism of the lads. There is frequent verbal, if not actual, violence shown to 'the fuckin' wogs' or the 'bastard pakis'. A clear demarcation between groups and a derogatory view of other racial types is simply assumed as the basis for this and other action: it is a daily form of knowledge in use.
8 For Willis, then, education is implicated in producing inequality. He argues that the 'reproduction' perspective neglects consciousness and culture and that his own approach is based on cultural studies – an approach which deals with how social agents are 'connected with' structure. Basing his work on the concept of 'cultural production' (the process of the collective creative use of discourses) he focuses on meaning and sense making. For Willis neither structure nor agency is understandable alone; there has to be some kind of dialectical relation between 'subjects formed in struggle and resistance to structures in domination, and structures formed in and reproduced by struggle and resistance against domination'. See Paul Willis, 'Cultural production and theories of reproduction', in Len Barton and Stephen Walker

(eds), *Race, Class and Education*, London, Croom Helm, 1983.

9 Some recent American sociologists of education like Anyon, Apple and Giroux, in contrast with deterministic structuralist writers, tend to be voluntaristic. They have a belief in testing theory by their empirical research, and vice versa. But they are intellectually and methodogically pluralist and their eclecticism often leads them to overlook incompatibilities. See Michael Apple, *Ideology and Curriculum*, London, Routledge & Kegan Paul, 1982; Henry Giroux, *Ideology, Culture and the Process of Schooling*, Lewes, Falmer Press, 1981.

10 Jean Anyon, 'Social class and the hidden curriculum of work', *Journal of Education*, vol. 162, no. 1, 1980, pp. 67–92.

11 A. Rampton, *West Indian Children in our Schools*, London, HMSO, 1981.

12 Ivor Morrish, *The Background of Immigrant Children*, London, Allen & Unwin, 1971. Quoted by Hazel Carby, 'Schooling in Babylon', in Centre for Contemporary Cultural Studies, *The Empire Strikes Back: Race and Racism in 70s Britain*, London, Hutchinson, 1982, p. 189.

13 Dawn Gill, *Assessment in a Multicultural Society, Schools Council Report: Geography*, London, Commission for Racial Equality, 1982. (See chapter 1, note 9).

14 There is a brilliant discussion about the exploitation of the 'Third World' in David Hare's play *A Map of the World*.

15 Jean Anyon, 'Ideology and United States history textbooks', in Roger Dale et al., *Education and the State, Volume 2: Politics, Patriarchy and Practice*, Lewes, Falmer Press, 1981.

16 See Madan Sarup, *Marxism/Structuralism/Education: Theoretical Developments in Sociology of Education*, Lewes, Falmer Press, 1983.

17 See the essay by Philip Wexler, 'Structure, text, and subject: a critical sociology of school knowledge', in Michael Apple (ed.), *Cultural and Economic Reproduction in Education*, London, Routledge & Kegan Paul, 1982.

18 Michael Apple, 'Curricular form and the logic of technical control', in Apple, op. cit., p. 261.

19 See the very useful, practical book by David Hicks, *Minorities: A Teacher's Resource Book for the Multi-ethnic Curriculum*, London, Heinemann Educational, 1981, p. 48.

20 Nicos Poulantzas, *State, Power, Socialism*, London, New Left Books, 1978.

21 Stuart Hall et al., *Policing the Crisis: Mugging, the State and Law and Order*, London, Macmillan, 1978.

Chapter 6 White feminism, black women and schooling

1 Michael Foucault, 'The discourse on language'. This is an appendix to the American edition of Michael Foucault, *The Archaeology of Knowledge*, New York, Pantheon, 1972.

2 For a clear introduction to these ideas see Alan Sheridan, *Michael Foucault, The Will to Truth*, London, Tavistock, 1980, p. 127.

3 Madeleine MacDonald (now Arnot), 'Socio-cultural reproduction and women's education', in Rosemary Deem (ed.), *Schooling for Women's Work*, London, Routledge & Kegan Paul, 1980. See also her article 'Schooling and the reproduction of class and gender relations', in Len Barton, Roland Meighan and Stephen Walker (eds), *Schooling, Ideology and the Curriculum*, Lewes, Falmer Press, 1980.

4 I am thinking of books like Eileen Byrne, *Women and Education*, London, Tavistock, 1978. When she wrote it she was education officer to the Equal Opportunities Commission.

5 See, for example, Dale Spender, and Elizabeth Sarah (eds), *Learning to Lose: Sexism and Education*, London, The Women's Press, 1980.

6 It is often said that the family and the education system are used in concert to sustain and reproduce the social and economic status quo. Specifically, they maintain existing relations within the family and social relations with the economy – what has sometimes been called the sexual and social division of labour. See Miriam David, *The State, the Family and Education*, London, Routledge & Kegan Paul, 1980.

7 In 1981 one in seven, approximately 15% of all families in Great Britain with dependent children (that is, under 16 years of age) were headed by a single parent. The great majority, around 90%, were headed by women. See *Social Trends* 15, Section 2, Tables 2–5 and subsequent discussion, Central Statistical Office, London, HMSO, 1985.

8 See Annette Kuhn and Ann Marie Wolpe (eds), *Feminism and Materialism*, London, Routledge & Kegan Paul, 1978, chapters 7 and 8.

9 Hazel Carby, '"White woman, listen": black feminism and the boundaries of sisterhood', in Centre for Contemporary Cultural Studies, *The Empire Strikes Back: Race and Racism in 70s Britain*, London, Hutchinson, 1982.

10 Ibid., p. 219.

11 Ibid., p. 221.

12 Angela McRobbie, 'Working class girls and the culture of femininity', in Women's Studies Group, Centre for Contemporary Cultural Studies, *Women Take Issue*, London, Hutchinson, 1978.

13 Just two examples: 'Though I could not include girls in the focus of this research, the approach outlined here is equally applicable, at least at a formal level, to the study of girls in school.' Paul Willis, *Learning to Labour*, Farnborough, Saxon House, 1977, p. 159. And: 'Our treatment of the themes of race and gender . . . is clearly inadequate.' Education Group, Centre for Contemporary Cultural Studies, *Unpopular Education*, London, Hutchinson, 1981, p. 8.

14 Mary Fuller, 'Black girls in an London comprehensive school', in Deem, op. cit. Fuller is critical of sociologists that marginalize or ignore women and of research that presents girls as uncritical 'conformists'. It should be mentioned, in passing, that both McRobbie and Fuller are white researchers.

15 Mary Fuller, 'Qualified criticism, critical qualifications', in Len Barton and Stephen Walker (eds), *Race, Class and Education*, London,

Croom Helm, 1983, p. 180.
16 The school achievement of girls of West Indian origin seems to be slightly superior to that of West Indian boys, and black women tend to outnumber men in education. This fact seems to contradict the 'double oppression' faced by black women. One wonders whether schools look more favourably on black girls as being potentially less disruptive than black boys?

Chapter 7   Black youth, schooling and unemployment

1 A. Sivanandan, *A Different Hunger: Writings on Black Resistance*, London, Pluto Press, 1982.
2 S. Castles and G. Kosack, *Immigrant Workers in the Class Structure in Western Europe*, Oxford, Oxford University Press, 1973. André Gorz has pointed out that 'the import of "ready-made" workers amounts to a saving, for the country of immigration, of between £8,000 and £16,000 per immigrant worker, if the social cost of a man is estimated for Western European countries as between five and ten years of work.' See André Gorz, 'The role of immigrant labour', *New Left Review*, no. 61, 1970.
3 This may be one of the effects of the micro-electronic revolution. Whereas in the past additional investment made for a growing number of jobs, at present it abolishes more jobs than it generates. Each job created for the construction of robots abolishes five jobs in the rest of the engineering industry. Gorz believes that the demand for more disposable time and better facilities to put it to a gratifying and creative use could be greatly helped by automation. He hopes for a planned redistribution of the shrinking amount of wage labour required so that everyone may work *and* work less and less while enjoying a guaranteed income. See André Gorz, *Farewell to the Working Class*, London, Pluto Press, 1983.
4 Manpower Services Commission, *Youth and Work*, The *Guardian* of 12 September 1983 said, 'Using Department of Education figures, the Runnymede Trust's latest bulletin shows that black unemployment over the past ten years has risen by more than 500 per cent, compared with a 300 per cent increase in unemployment generally. In 1981, 17.2 per cent of blacks were unemployed, compared to 9.9 per cent of the working population generally.'
5 John Rex's work includes: *Race Relations in Sociological Theory*, London, Weidenfeld & Nicholson, 1970; *Race, Colonialism and the City*, London, Routledge & Kegan Paul, 1973; *Colonial Immigrants in a British City*, London, Routledge & Kegan Paul, 1979.
6 Ernest Mandel, *Late Capitalism*, London, New Left Books, 1975, chapter 8.
    Though the growing structural unemployment is partly caused by the increasing use of micro-electronics, there is still a lack of socialist analysis and technology. Perhaps this is because in the past marxists

have concentrated on an analysis of distribution rather than production. The pervasive view is that science and technology is being used not only because it increases productivity, but because it increases social control. Workers are becoming deskilled, knowledge is being objectified, human intelligence is being suppressed. In the office, for example, there is to be no more walking, talking, thinking or dreaming. Why is the government cutting the number of university places and hospital beds and is yet providing computers for every school? I would argue that science and technology reflect the values of society. What, then, are the assumptions built into the new technology? Predictability, repeatability, replicability. These, the characteristics of Western capitalist science, are also the characteristics of Taylorism, of scientific management. But what about intuition? What about the imagination? And if we believe that control should reside with the worker, the problem is this: can technology be human-centred, designed according to socialist criteria?

7 Harry Braverman, *Labor and Monopoly Capital*, New York, Monthly Review Press, 1975, p. 256.

8 Geoff Hunt and Jenny Mellor, 'Afro-Caribbean youth: racism and unemployment', in Mike Cole and Bob Skelton (eds), *Blind Alley: Youth in a Crisis of Capital*, Ormskirk, G.W. and H. Hesketh, 1980, p. 58.

9 'An ideology always exists in an apparatus and its practice, or practices. This existence is material.' Louis Althusser, 'Ideology and ideological state apparatuses', in B.R. Cosin (ed.), *Education: Structure and Society*, Harmondsworth, Penguin, 1972, p. 267. For a discussion of Althusser and the problems and advances in the theory of ideology see Paul Hirst, *On Law and Ideology*, London, Macmillan, 1979, esp. chapter 2.

10 Malcolm Cross, 'The manufacture of marginality', in Ernest Cashmore and Barry Troyna (eds), *Black Youth in Crisis*, London, Allen & Unwin, 1982, p. 51.

11 'Seventeen teenagers have died and 700 been seriously injured while working on Youth Opportunities Programme schemes during the three years of the programme.' *Guardian*, 14 July, 1983, p. 6.

12 Education Group, Centre for Contemporary Cultural Studies, *Unpopular Education: Schooling and Social democracy in England since 1944*, London, Hutchinson, 1981, p. 238. See also the useful article by Andy Green, 'Education and training: under new masters', in Ann-Marie Wolpe and James Donald (eds), *Is there Anyone Here from Education?*, London, Pluto Press, 1983.

13 'The stability of monopoly capitalism vitally depends on the relations between these two forces, the mental and manual, remaining safely divided. Should the division be changed into an alliance the authority of the management would be in jeopardy. Acting in unison the direct producers could dispose of the capitalist management and take production into their own control.' Alfred Sohn-Rethel, *Intellectual and Manual Labour*, London, Macmillan, 1978, p. 157. This is still the most thought-provoking book on the subject.

131

14 Paul Willis, *Learning to Labour,* Farnborough, Saxon House, 1977.
15 See Ken Browne, 'School, capitalism and the mental/manual division of labour', *Sociological Review,* vol. 29, no. 3, 1981, p. 468.
16 I am referring here to the 'correspondence' theory of Samuel Bowles and Herbert Gintis, *Schooling in Capitalist America,* London, Routledge & Kegan Paul, 1976.
17 This section draws on Paul Willis, 'Youth unemployment: thinking the unthinkable', *Youth and Policy,* vol. 2, no. 4, 1984.
18 Richard Johnson, ' "Really useful knowledge"; radical education and working-class culture, 1790–1848', in John Clarke et al. (eds), *Working-Class Culture,* London, Hutchinson, 1979, p. 95. The term 'really useful knowledge' was used as a way of distancing working-class aims from some immediate (capitalist) conception of utility and from recreational or divisionary notions. It expressed the conviction that real knowledge served practical ends, that politics and education went together in a complicated web of means-ends relationship. Education without politics was deemed inadequate; but politics without education was also inadequate. See also Richard Johnson, 'Notes on the schooling of the English working class, 1780–1850', in Roger Dale et al. (eds), *Schooling and Capitalism,* London, Routledge & Kegan Paul, 1976.

Chapter 8   Hegemony, race and class

1 The achievement and maintenance of hegemony is largely a matter of education. See James Joll, *Gramsci,* London, Fontana, 1977, pp. 93–102. Carl Boggs, *Gramsci's Marxism,* London, Pluto Press, 1976, p. 39.
2 Chantel Mouffe, *Gramsci and Marxist Theory,* London, Routledge & Kegan Paul, 1979, p. 182.
3 Perry Anderson, 'The antimonies of Antonio Gramsci', *New Left Review,* no. 100, 1976–7.
4 'Would a scholar at the age of forty be able to sit for sixteen hours on end at his worktable if he had not as a child, compulsorily, through mechanical coercion, acquired the appropriate psycho-physical habits?' Quinton Hoare and Geoffrey Nowell-Smith (eds), *Antonio Gramsci, Selections from the Prison Notebooks,* London, Lawrence & Wishart, 1971, p. 37.
5 Ibid., p. 350.
6 Ibid., p. 377. Gramsci reminds us that bourgeois ideas did not come readily packaged with capitalism. The bourgeoisie fought hard for its ideas in the 'hegemonic' battle against the old regime. Socialists must now struggle against the conservative views of the bourgeoisie.
7 *National-popular* refers to struggles common to more than one social class, fraction or group which can be strategically linked together. In Britain today this would include black men and women, unemployed youth, nuclear disarmament and women's groups. It is an important

concept because it recognizes the specificity of national conditions and traditions. It is the basis of the 1978 edition of the Communist Party's *The British Road to Socialism*. But does the concept involve a double ideological slide: national replacing international and popular replacing proletarian? The main problem is that there is often a narrow distinction between class alliances that are hegemonic for the working class and class alliances that can be tipped the other way and reorganized under the hegemony of the bourgeoisie. See David Forgacs, 'National-popular: genealogy of a concept', in *Formations Of Nation and People,* Routledge & Kegan Paul, 1984. For a useful, short account of Gramscian strategy see also John Molyneux, *Marxism and the Party,* London, Pluto Press, 1978, chapter 6.

8 Mouffe, op. cit., p. 189.
9 Ernesto Laclau, *Politics and Ideology in Marxist Theory,* London, New Left Books, 1977, p. 81.
10 Ibid., p. 99.
11 Ibid., p. 115.
12 Ibid., p. 160–1. Critics of this position argue that when socialism and nationalism are combined socialism is inevitably subordinated to nationalism.
13 Ibid., p. 196.
14 Ernesto Laclau, 'Populist rupture and discourse', *Screen Education,* no. 34, 1980, p. 87.
15 Some of these criticisms are made by Bob Jessop who holds that this 'novel account of hegemony must be adjudged partial and incomplete'. Bob Jessop, *The Capitalist State,* Oxford, Martin Robertson, 1982, pp. 192–202.
16 Mouffe, op. cit., p. 193.
17 But if the material disadvantages of the working class were eliminated, would the problem of working-class racism disappear? See Annie Phizacklea and Robert Miles, 'Working-class beliefs in the inner city', in Robert Miles and Annie Phizacklea (eds), *Racism and Political Action in Britain,* London, Routledge & Kegan Paul, 1979, p. 97. Miles believes that many writers, wanting to construct a theory of race relations, tend to reify 'race'. They use the term race as if it were real, forgetting that it is a taxonomic device, an abstraction, an ideology. There is no such thing as race; racism, however, exists and has effects.
18 A. Sivanandan, 'Challenging racism – a strategy for the 1980s', *Searchlight,* n. 95, 1983, p. 18.
19 This point is made by Tom Nairn, *The Break-Up of Britain,* London, New Left Books, 1977, p. 274.
20 A. Sivanandan has described how the state atomized the working class and created hierarchies within it based on race and nationality to make conflicting sectional interests assume greater significance than the interest of the class as a whole. See A. Sivanandan, *A Different Hunger: Writings on Black Resistance,* London, Pluto Press, 1982, p. 104.
21 Sally Tomlinson, 'Black women in higher education – case studies of university women in Britain', in Len Barton and Stephen Walker

(eds), *Race, Class and Education*, London, Croom Helm, 1983, p. 79. This book contains a most useful teaching bibliography.

22 B.M. Bullivant, *Race, Ethnicity and Curriculum*, Melbourne, Macmillan of Australia, 1981.

23 According to Chris Mullard a 'racial code' exists. The code seeks to produce (production), perpetuate (reproduction) and change (reaction) a racial construction of reality. I must admit that I do not find this level of abstraction very helpful and I am not sure of the value of arguing that such a thing as a 'racial code' exists. See Chris Mullard, 'The racial code: its features, rules and change', in Len Barton and Stephen Walker (eds), *Race, Class and Education*, London, Croom Helm, 1983.

24 Farrukh Dhondy, 'Teaching young blacks', *Race Today*, May/June 1978, pp. 80–5. But isn't this view rather limited? If Dhondy had 'resisted', could he have achieved the knowledge and power that he now has?

25 See, for example, Centre for Contemporary Cultural Studies, *The Empire Strikes Back: Race and Racism in 70s Britain*, London, Hutchinson, 1982.

26 I accept the fact that there are racial differences but I want to ask: why have some of these differences consistently become historically important? How have these differences been organized and mobilized in different societies at different stages of history?

Chapter 9 Conclusions . . .

1 One way in which schools are sponsoring black academic failure is through sport. There has been an upsurge of black involvement in sport at every level during the past decade in Britain. According to some recent research it has been found that West Indians are more likely to participate in extra-curricular sport and to play in sports teams than pupils of other ethnic groups. It seems that sport provides the school with a convenient and legitimate side track for its disillusioned black low achievers and as a social-control mechanism. The over-representation of Afro-Caribbean pupils in school sports teams is in part the outcome of channelling by teachers who have a tendency to view this ethnic group in stereotypical terms, as having skills of the body rather than skills of the mind. By encouraging these allegedly 'motor-minded' pupils to concentrate on sport in school at some expense to their academic studies, teachers have reinforced West Indian academic failure. See Bruce Carrington, 'Sport as a side track. An analysis of West Indian involvement in extra-curricular sport', in Len Barton and Stephen Walker (eds), *Race, Class and Education*, London, Croom Helm, 1983.

2 The main weakness of the social-democratic approach in the sociology of education is that it does not consider capital. Capitalism is

considered unproblematic and taken for granted; its requirements are ignored. The Social Democrats believe that change comes about through changing state policy, through social engineering. This is what Halsey, Vaizey and Crosland tried to do.

3 Jorge Lorrain, *The Concept of Ideology*, London, Hutchinson, 1979, p. 210.

4 The utter irrationality of capitalist production as a mode of satisfying human needs is the thesis of Geoffrey Kay, *The Economic Theory of the Working Class*, London, Macmillan, 1979. Other useful books on marxist economics include: Geoffrey Kay, *Development and Underdevelopment, A Marxist Analysis*, London, Macmillan, 1975; Ben Fine and Laurence Harris, *Rereading Capital*, London, Macmillan 1979.

5 The state does three things: it aids accumulation; it provides a context in which accumulation can go forward in an unhindered way – a form of social control; and it provides legitimation – this is done by concealing the activities of capital and makes them appear unpolitical. As it is not possible for the state to do all these things at the same time, contradictions become manifest. See the excellent reader by David Held et al. (eds), *States and Societies*, Oxford, Martin Robertson, 1983.

6 Robert Jeffcoate, *Positive Image; Towards a Multi-Racial Curriculum*, London, Writers' and Readers' Publishing Co-operative/Chameleon Books, 1979.

7 Gerald Grace, *Teachers, Ideology and Control: A Study in Urban Education*, London, Routledge & Kegan Paul, 1978, p. 13.

8 See Caroline Benn, 'Independence and accountability for all', in AnnMarie Wolpe and James Donald (eds), *Is There Anyone Here From Education?*, London, Pluto Press, 1983.

Chapter 10   . . . and beginnings

1 Brian Salter and Ted Tapper, *Education, Politics and the State*, London, Grant McIntyre, 1983.

2 See Roger Dale, 'The political sociology of education', *British Journal of Sociology of Education*, vol. 4, no. 2, 1983, p. 185. For a clear introduction to the theories of the state see Bob Jessop, *The Capitalist State*, Oxford, Martin Robertson, 1982.

3 There are some exceptions. One of them is the Inner London Education Authority which is currently taking steps to eliminate racism from the education service. It has formulated guidelines for schools and colleges. Information is available from ILEA, County Hall, London SE1 7PB.

4 Again I am thinking of Hegel's story about the Master and the Slave; see Alexandre Kojève, *Introduction to the Reading of Hegel*, assembled by Raymond Queneau, New York, Basic Books, 1969.

5 But freeing oneself completely from Western cultural beliefs and

thought may be neither possible nor desirable. And it is difficult to fight the (Western) Master's cultural hegemony without using tools derived from that same tradition. In a sense the education of black people has meaning only in relation to the other from which it wishes to distinguish itself. This is an ambiguous relationship because the assertion of one's difference often goes hand in hand with an urge to have it recognized by the Other.

6 The Scarman Report, *The Brixton Disorders 10th–12th April, 1981*, Harmondsworth, Penguin, 1982.

7 See the remarkable book by Paulin Hountondji, *African Philosophy*, London, Hutchinson, 1983.

8 A good introduction to this topic is Richard Norman and Sean Sayers, *Hegel, Marx and Dialectic*, Hassocks, Sussex, Harvester Press, 1980.

9 Alfred Schmidt, *The Concept of Nature in Marx*, London, New Left Books, 1971.

10 Let me give an example of what I mean: here is a brief précis of what students might learn in an integrated social science course entitled *Imperialism in the Silicon Age*.

From a system in which labour moved to the centres of capital, imperalism has developed into a system in which capital moves to wherever there is an accessible source of cheap labour. This process has been accelerated by the new industrial revolution based on microelectronics. Changes of such magnitude and speed have never been experienced before.

This new industrial revolution, like the old, has taken off on the backs of the workers in the peripheries. The multinationals at first used Hong Kong, Taiwan, South Korea and Singapore. They are now using Malaysia, Thailand, the Philippines, Indonesia and Sri Lanka.

Development in these countries is *disorganic,* that is to say, the economic system is at odds with the cultural and political institutions of the people it exploits. The economic system is not mediated by culture or legitimated by politics as it is in the advanced capitalist countries.

What has capitalist development meant for the masses of the countries mentioned above? Only increased poverty, repressive regimes and the corruption of their cultures. But as the base and superstructure are in fundamental conflict in these countries, this contradiction often develops into a conflict between the political regime and the people.

The points are from A. Sivanandan, 'Imperialism and disorganic development in the silicon age', in *A Different Hunger: Writings on Black Resistance*, London, Pluto Press, 1982. See also Anthony Brewer, *Marxist Theories of Imperialism*, London, Routledge & Kegan Paul, 1982.

11 Stuart Hall, *Drifting into a Law and Order Society,* London, Cobden Trust, 1980 (obtainable from the Cobden Trust, 21 Tabard Street, London SE1 4LA); Edward Thompson, *Writing by Candlelight,* London, Merlin, 1980. See also 'The secret state', *State Research Pamphlet,* no. 1., 1979, and 'Policing the eighties',· *State Research Pamphlet,* no. 2, 1981.

12 Bob Fine, 'Law, order and police powers', in D. Coates and G. Johnstone (eds), *Arguments for Socialists,* London, Martin Robertson, 1983.

Index